ESUS **ANSWERING** SAID
HE LAW OF **THE** LORD, AND
AND **TOUGHEST** OF HIDE
MORE **QUESTIONS** THE
E IS **ABOUT** TO FILL HIS S
PIRIT OF **GOD** WAS HOVE
R FATHER **AND** THE LORD
E ON **THE BIBLE** THEIR L

ANSWERING THE TOUGHEST QUESTIONS ABOUT GOD AND THE BIBLE

BRUCE BICKEL
& STAN JANTZ

WITH CHRISTOPHER GREER

BETHANYHOUSE
a division of Baker Publishing Group
Minneapolis, Minnesota

Published by Bethany House Publishers
11400 Hampshire Avenue South
Bloomington, Minnesota 55438
www.bethanyhouse.com

Bethany House Publishers is a division of
Baker Publishing Group, Grand Rapids, Michigan

Printed in the United States of America

Library of Congress Control Number: 2016938465

ISBN 978-0-7642-1870-5

Cover design by Rob Williams, InsideOutCreativeArts

Authors are represented by The Steve Laube Agency

16 17 18 19 20 21 22   7 6 5 4 3 2 1

Contents

Acknowledgments

Bruce and Stan want to thank Christopher Greer for the work he contributed to this book. In addition to conducting countless personal interviews and designing the surveys, he helped outline and write several chapters.

Bruce, Stan, and Chris want to acknowledge the many young adults—especially those from St. Andrew's Presbyterian Church in Newport Beach, California—who took the time to articulate their most important questions about God and the Bible. The questions you asked show that you really want to know.

Introduction

The world is full of questions. Whether the topic is politics, race, relationships, the environment, or religion (especially religion), there seem to be more questions than answers.

That's not a bad thing. In fact, it's quite good. In past generations, asking questions was considered rude or disrespectful, especially when it came to God and the Bible. "God said it, I believe it, that settles it for me" was the response Christians were supposed to have. Anything more and you were labeled a Doubting Thomas. People who weren't among the faithful were reluctant to ask questions about God out of concern they would be considered un-American (we're not kidding).

How things have changed.

These days, people are not shy about questioning God and the Bible. Some doubt God's existence, others question his goodness, and many are troubled by the attitudes and behaviors of those who claim to follow him. Many Christians have some of the same questions and concerns.

Far from being a worrisome trend, we think tough questions about God and the Bible are exactly what we need to gain an appreciation and even a love for God. We even like it when people doubt whether God and his story are true. Not only does such doubt lead to great questions; doubt leads to sound belief. In fact, without doubt, there is no faith.

Questions and doubt are part of the biblical story. Here are just a few of the doubters who populate the pages of Scripture:

- Abraham doubted that God would give him a son.
- Moses questioned God's choosing him to bring God's people out of Egypt.
- Thomas doubted the reality of the risen Christ.

In each instance, God extended grace. He was patient rather than punitive with those who doubted and asked serious questions. Unfortunately, those of us who claim to know God personally haven't always shown the same grace and patience.

As you will read in chapter 1, we were inspired to write this book by a remark made by a young Christian who wasn't given "space" to express his doubts and ask his questions. Moved by his sincerity, we decided to write a book designed to open the doors of conversation and encourage people to wrestle with the toughest questions about God and the Bible with grace, humility, truth, and love.

If you're going to write a book that answers the toughest questions about God and the Bible, you need to know what those questions are. And the only way to know is to ask. Thankfully, we weren't alone in the process. Christopher Greer, a pastor who ministers primarily to young adults, helped us immensely. Over a period of several months, he asked people individually and in small group settings, as well as through a comprehensive online survey. Chris talked with a lot of people, all with the same goal: What are the questions about God and the Bible you struggle with the most?

The results were both gratifying and humbling. We were grateful that people opened up and asked honest, probing questions. These weren't theoretical questions. They were personal. People really wanted to know.

We were also humbled, because these are not easy questions. The ten questions that rose to the top of the conversations and surveys—the ten questions we consider in this book—go to the heart of who God is and what he has said to us in his Word.

Our intention in this book is to do more than answer the toughest questions about God and the Bible. As much as possible, we hope this book helps you—whether you are addressing questions you have had for years, or exploring these issues for the first time—connect with God on a deeper and more meaningful level than ever before.

Bruce Bickel and Stan Jantz

1

Is God Real, and How Can You Know?

Introduction

Every book needs inspiration. It can come from the author's personal experience, or it can be something external, like an event, an article, or even a headline. For us, it was a headline from a letter that drew us in: "Confessions of an Ex-Evangelical, Pro-SSM Millennial."

As we read the letter, posted by a popular blogger who left the letter writer anonymous, we were inspired to write our book in a certain way. The letter, written by a twenty-four-year-old who grew up in an evangelical church—and eventually left the faith of his childhood after his views on gay rights changed—did more than inspire us. It helped shape the tone of this book. Here's the part of this young adult's letter that got to us:

> My leaving was much more about what the gay rights issues revealed about that faith than it was about the actual issue of gays and their right to marry. . . .

We were taught that our church not only had the absolute truth, but that there was no earthly history between the Bible and the doctrines being presented to us. . . . I cannot for the life of me remember once when the name of a theologian was mentioned. There was one interpretation of scripture, and it was absolutely true. . . .

The problem these churches inevitably run into with their young members and same sex marriage is on the issue of doubt. When you have a feelings based salvation in a faith in which doubt is a sign of spiritual failure, the young members of these churches lack the space to wrestle with a tough issue like this.[1]

The last twelve words of the letter were the most powerful and convicting of all. We realize not all churches fall into the category described by this young adult, but arguably it characterizes many churches. And it's not just "young members" who are discouraged by the lack of space to wrestle with doubt. We suspect most churchgoers are dismayed by this reality.

We don't pretend to have all the answers, and we are certainly not a church, but we are prepared to provide a space to wrestle with doubt. We realize there are limitations. We can't actually talk to you, but we have heard you (or at least people like you), and we have done our best to ask some of the questions you are asking about God and the Bible. And while we have provided some answers to these important questions, we hope we leave enough space for you to wrestle and to keep asking.

Is God real? And how can you know? Nothing like starting with the most important questions anyone can ask, right? And since they are almost impossible to answer with absolute certainty, let's just call it a day and move on to the next question.

Just kidding.

Let's camp on these two questions for a while. After all, they are questions you will come back to again . . . and again . . . and again . . . until you are satisfied you have an answer. And though

God is not a simple, measurable, physical object that can be contained and tested (he is God, for crying out loud), there are no greater questions to wrestle with.

Certainty, Doubt, and Belief

We've become so accustomed to analyzing God, trying to figure him out, and coming to conclusions about him that we've pretty much lost perspective on a Being who

1. created the universe out of nothing;
2. knows everything that's going on in the universe he made; and
3. knows everything about you, including how many hairs you have on your head. (We're not making that up—it really does say that in the Bible.)

With all that in mind (and that's just scratching the surface), do we really think we can quantify God, put borders around him, and come up with a "final answer" about his existence? Not really. Of course, you can conclude that he doesn't exist. But arriving at that conclusion is no picnic, either. *Not* believing in God is subject to the same kinds of limitations as believing in God.

The Problem With Certainty

The thing is, a lot of people throughout history have tried to button down an answer to the question of whether God does or doesn't exist. Until a few years ago, those who believed in God didn't have to back up their belief because nobody challenged the idea that God is real.

It used to be that belief in God was accepted without question. The only people who challenged the reality of God were obnoxious atheists or existential European philosophers. Few people wanted to be associated with either group, so belief in God was the default position for just about everyone.

Then things changed. Interesting and intelligent atheists began to openly challenge the notion that there is a God, which forced thinking Christians to view their faith as more than the summary of their emotions and heritage. In our view, this has been a positive and much-needed development. What good is having a belief if you don't know why you believe it or, more importantly, why it matters? But that's what happens when no one challenges what you believe. You get complacent. You get soft. There's no passion. There's no meaning.

A New Kind of Atheism

What changed was a new kind of atheism. Instead of obnoxious people saying, "God is dead," you had intelligent, articulate, normal people saying, "God isn't real." And they made a compelling case, usually from the perspective of science, but sometimes for no other reason than they felt betrayed and deceived by the church they grew up in (like the Ex-Evangelical, Pro-SSM Millennial).

These "new atheists," brimming with confidence as their numbers grew and public opinion started turning their way, began putting people of faith into a "special" category. They started treating Christians like children. Oh, they had their rational arguments against God's existence, but the most damaging approach had nothing to do with reason and more to do with labeling people of faith as emotional, less intelligent, and naïve.

Now, in defense of people who don't believe in God, not all of them take such a dim view of people who believe. And there was a time when people of faith put the same kind of label on atheists. But now the tables have turned. People who don't believe are on the offensive, and those who believe in God have been forced to get defensive.

- On a scale of 1 to 10—with 1 being "I don't believe in God at all" and 10 being "God said it, I believe it, that settles it for me"—where do you see yourself right now?
- If you believe in God, how do you feel when you're around people who don't believe?
- If you struggle to believe in God, or have serious doubts about what you believe, what is your view of Christians who seem so sure of their beliefs?
- What problems has this "spiritual certainty" created for people who are still on a search for God?

Apologetics Fires Back

As you might expect, some Christians were not about to take this challenge from the new atheists without a fight. So along came the modern apologetics movement, which is basically about defending your faith. (Just to clarify, people who study and use apologetics aren't *apologizing* for what they believe. They are simply *giving answers* for the common questions about the reality of God.)

Apologetics as a *tool* can be useful, and the field certainly attracts its share of people who want buttoned-down answers to perplexing questions. The problem is that, for the most part, studying apologetics gives you the ability to *answer* the questions people are asking about God and the Christian story, rather than teaching you to actually *listen* to the people who are asking the questions. We can't speak for all Christian apologists, but you get the impression that this approach is based on trying to *prove* God exists so that reasonable people will see the light, believe in God, and soon become Christians.

Despite the fine work being done in the field of Christian apologetics, you have to wonder how effective it has been. Based on the evidence of changed lives, there doesn't appear to be a huge number of new converts flooding churches because suddenly there are a whole bunch of answers to questions about God. In fact, just the opposite is true. Overall, church attendance is declining as more and more people look for answers and meaning *outside* the church, mainly because most churches have not provided a place for people to wrestle with the toughest questions about God and the Bible.

Somewhere in the Middle

While it may seem as though people who have left the church are skeptics, we haven't found that to be the case. In our experience, these "leavers" are somewhere in the middle, between unbelief and belief, between outright skepticism and absolute certainty. They haven't arrived at a place where they believe the Christian story, but neither have they embraced unbelief. They're in the middle. They have thought enough about this whole God thing to realize two very important principles:

- No amount of evidence can prove beyond a shadow of a doubt that God exists.
- No amount of evidence can prove beyond a shadow of a doubt that God doesn't exist.

The way we see it, all of us, even those of us who haven't left the church, are somewhere on a continuum between outright skepticism and absolute certainty. We call this the *Doubt Continuum*.

Interpreting the Doubt Continuum

We're not social scientists (like that wasn't obvious), but we are fascinated by human nature and belief. Plus we have a secret weapon— a young pastor and young adult leader (that would be Chris) who has been researching the questions people are asking. We think our Doubt Continuum accurately reflects the range in which most people find themselves when it comes to doubt and belief.

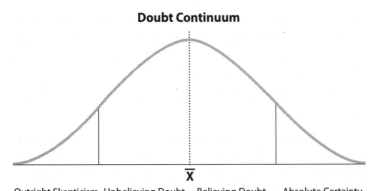

Doubt Continuum

Outright Skepticism   Unbelieving Doubt   Believing Doubt   Absolute Certainty

X = Believing God by trusting in Jesus Christ

The shape of the Doubt Continuum illustrates that the vast majority of people are bunched on either side of the dotted line that represents the act of trusting God by faith. Some would call this line *conversion*. Others would be comfortable labeling it *accepting Jesus into your heart*. Let's just say this line is a time—although it doesn't have to be a precise *moment* in time (that's why it's a dotted line)—when a person makes a decision to surrender to God and accept the path to salvation. Essentially, this means believing by faith that we can have a relationship with God if we accept his rescue plan to save us through Jesus.

QUESTIONS FOR REFLECTION AND DISCUSSION

- Why do you think more people than ever are leaving the church to look for answers to life's most important questions?
- Has there been a time in your life when you trusted Jesus and became a Christian? Describe what that process was like.

What About That Doubt?

Okay, it's time to put your mind at ease when it comes to doubt. Doubt isn't a bad thing. Doubt is a useful emotion for skeptics and believers alike. Take a look at our Doubt Continuum again. Notice that there's doubt on both sides of the dotted line. So what's the difference?

Unbelieving doubt: struggling to accept a God who seems to be a jerk

People on the left side of the dotted line—except for the outright skeptics—probably aren't struggling with God's existence. They believe God exists, but they aren't sure what to make of him. For them, it's often a question of God's *goodness*. Their doubts swirl around their perception that God isn't what he says he is. God claims to be loving, faithful, true, and good. But if that's the case, why is there so much suffering and evil in the world?

The struggle for doubting unbelievers is between a God who is supposed to be loving and a world he made that includes a lot of really bad stuff. If God is so good, why won't he deal with suffering and evil?

Essentially, they believe that God is real, but they don't like the reality. It would be as if you finally got to meet your favorite celebrity, only to discover that he or she is a total jerk. You don't stop believing that the celebrity exists, but your dreams about having a close and meaningful relationship with that celebrity vanish when you actually see him or her in the real world.

So the doubts about God continue to build, not because you don't believe he exists, but because you want nothing to do with a God you think is a jerk.

For people who do not yet believe God enough to trust him with their lives, their doubts are more *intellectual* than emotional. They know enough about God to spark inquiry, but not enough to help them come to an understanding of his character and the way he works in the world. Even more to the point, they don't *know* God personally. They don't understand certain things about God because they don't yet understand God.

Of course, nobody knows and understands God completely, and even an entry-level understanding of God takes time, just like it takes time to get to know anyone. But as we get to know God better, we understand him more and are troubled by him less.

Believing doubt: struggling to trust a God who doesn't seem to deliver on his promises

People on the right side of the dotted line have different kinds of doubts. They have made the decision to trust Jesus. But when God doesn't answer their prayers, and their problems continue, they start wondering (and doubting) if God is all he's cracked up to be. They can't see past their disappointment with God.

Whereas unbelieving doubt is more intellectual in nature, believing doubt is more *emotional*. Disappointment, disillusionment, discouragement—these are all emotions. There's a tendency for us to focus on our own weakness rather than on God's strength, and this leads to fear. Sometimes, rather than hiding behind our doubts, we need to get past our fear by exercising some faith and trusting God for the courage and wisdom to get through the valley we are in.

QUESTIONS FOR REFLECTION AND DISCUSSION

- Describe a time when you were profoundly disappointed with God. What happened?
- How did you deal with your disappointment?
- Once you got through it, did you learn anything about God that you didn't know before?

When Doubt Helps

God isn't surprised when people doubt him. It doesn't even bother him. How do we know this? Because of the way Jesus treated one of his disciples, famously (or infamously) known as Doubting

Thomas. Jesus had been crucified, was dead and buried. But he rose again and appeared to more than five hundred people, including his disciples—except for one. It seems Thomas was missing when Jesus first appeared to his followers, and even though his colleagues told Thomas about the risen Lord, he refused to believe. "Unless I see the nail marks in his hands and put my finger where the nails were, and put my hand into his side, I will not believe" (John 20:25). Talk about a tough sell!

A week later, Jesus appeared before his disciples again, and this time Thomas was with them. Rather than scold the doubting disciple, Jesus invited him to examine the nail holes in his hands and the wound in his side. "Stop doubting and believe," Jesus told Thomas (verse 27).

Thomas did indeed believe (who wouldn't at that point?), which prompted Jesus to make a profound observation. "Because you have seen me, you have believed," he said to Thomas. "Blessed are those who have not seen and yet have believed" (verse 29).

That's us, folks. We have not seen, yet Jesus says if we believe, we are blessed. In effect, Jesus is saying that our doubts are useful because they guide us to a truth that is as much subjective and mysterious as it is objective and empirical. There are facts concerning the historicity of Jesus, but we weren't there like Thomas was. We can know Jesus is risen, and we can believe God is real, but it's not with 100 percent certainty because we haven't actually *seen* him.

And that's just where God wants us.

You see, believing in God is more than believing objective facts about God. It's great that there are plenty of clues in the universe and throughout history that point to the existence of God. But clues and facts alone don't tell the whole story. Belief is more than coming to conclusions. Even the devils of hell have concluded that God exists (James 2:19). True belief happens only when it leads to trust, and trust is valid only when the object of your trust is worthy of your belief.

- Many of those who saw Jesus firsthand and witnessed his miracles (including the resurrection) did not believe in him. Why do you think that was the case?
- Why is it better to believe when you can't see?

You Won't Believe What You Don't Trust

You can believe all you want that an airplane is going to fly. But unless the airplane has fuel and a trained and trustworthy pilot in the cockpit, no amount of belief is going to get that airplane off the ground. The same principle (only on a much grander scale) applies to God. If you can't trust him, you won't believe.

At its core, *trust* is directly related to *truth*. You don't trust something because it's false. You trust something—whether an object such as an airplane, or a scientific theory, or another human being—if it's rooted in truth. At the first sign that truth has been compromised, your trust goes away. The same principle (only on a much grander scale) applies to God. If he isn't true, if he's just made up, then there's no reason at all to trust him. By the same token, the only reason to become a Christian is to believe that the Christian story is true.

With the exception of the Bible, C. S. Lewis is arguably the world's most quoted Christian writer. That's because he always seems to get to the heart of the matter when it comes to believing in God and the Christian story. Here is one of his better-known statements about Christianity, and why you should believe or disbelieve it:

> Christianity claims to give an account of the facts—to tell you what the real universe is like. Its account of the universe may be true, or it may not, and once that question is really before you, then your natural inquisitiveness must make you want to know the answer. If Christianity is untrue, then no honest man will want to believe

it, however helpful it may be: if it is true, every honest man will want to believe it, even if it gives him no help at all.[2]

Let's Review

We've reached the halfway point of this first chapter. Let's pause for a brief review of how doubt, belief, and trust all enter into the process of determining whether or not God is real.

- *Doubt* is a necessary part of life because you will never have absolute certainty in most things (how's that for an absolutely certain statement?). When it comes to belief in God, this is especially applicable on both sides of the Doubt Continuum. You can't be absolutely certain God exists, and you can't say for sure that he doesn't.

- *Belief* is easy when you can experience something with one of your five senses. But when you can't detect or inspect something with your eyes, ears, nose, hands, or tongue, belief gets trickier. It takes faith to believe something you can't experience personally. But is it *blind* faith? It depends. Blind faith is believing in something you know nothing about. *True* faith is based on your knowing that something has good reason to be real or true (remember our example of the pilot and the airplane?).

  When it comes to the reality of God, belief and faith work together to give you the confidence that God exists (the word *confidence* literally means "with faith"). Yet there's one more step you need to take. You need to *trust* the object of your belief.

- *Trust* comes into play when you commit yourself to something you believe to be true (like physically boarding an airplane). When you put your trust in God, you not only believe that he exists, but are also willing to live as if that is true.

24

But we're getting ahead of ourselves. Before we can talk about trusting in God, we need to look more closely at the second question posed in this chapter.

How Can We Know God Is Real?

When we talk about something being real, what we mean is this: Is it true? By its very definition, truth is anything that corresponds to reality. It's something you *know* to be true. So to answer the question "How can we know God is real?" we have to ask two other questions:

- Can we know God exists?
- Can we know God?

The first question goes to *evidence*, or *objective* reality. The second question goes to *experience*, or *subjective* reality. The same principle applies to people. Think about someone, whether they are living now or lived in the past. You can know objectively that this person exists (or existed), but that doesn't necessarily mean you *know* the person.

For each of these questions, we will provide a "framework of discovery" so you can approach some possible answers. Are you ready? Let's dig in.

Can We Know God Exists?

As you wrestle with this important question, here are three things to consider:

1. Just because God can't be detected by any of the five senses doesn't mean you can't discover the truth about God. An emotion such as love can't be measured by any one of the senses, but we know love exists. How? Because we can see love

25

in action. We can measure the effects of love on ourselves and on others. Same thing is true of historical figures. You can't detect Abraham Lincoln with your senses, but you know he existed because of the evidence.

2. There's no "smoking gun" kind of evidence that "proves" God exists, but there is evidence, and there are reasonable assumptions you can make based on that evidence. You can't say, "I know for sure that God exists," but you can say, "It is reasonable to believe that God exists." Is that good enough? That's for you to determine.

3. We're going to outline three of the most common evidences, or reasons, for the existence of God. As we said, none of these is a smoking gun, but each one has merit. Not everyone will agree on the strength of any one piece of evidence. Something you find compelling may be a weak argument for someone else. So instead of focusing on one piece of evidence or argument, look at these as multiple clues leading you to uncover a mystery. Any one clue may not be enough to stand on its own, but the cumulative weight of all three clues may just add up to a reasonable case for the existence of God.

Okay, let's look at three clues, each followed by a question. Do your best to discuss and answer each question.

Clue #1: CONTINGENCY—Why is there something rather than nothing?

How do you answer this? Think of any object around you, such as the chair you're sitting in, your phone, or the bird flying past your window. Why do these things exist? Think about just one object. What were the steps it took to bring that object to its present form?

This sequence of steps preceding any object relates to the idea of *contingency*, which basically means this: *Anything that exists is contingent upon something else.* That's a reasonable statement, but there's just one problem. You can't have an endless series of contingent things. At some point, the process has to start with something that isn't contingent. If this were not the case, the object you are thinking of—the chair, your phone, the bird—would never come into existence.

This is known as the "impossibility of crossing infinity." In the language of mathematics, it means, "Infinite regression is impossible." Put another way, to get to a *present* thing, you must have a *first* thing. Even Steve Jobs, as good as he was at coming up with great ideas that led to great products, had a mother!

With this in mind, here's another question to ponder: How many *first* things can there be in the natural world? Put another way, is there anything in the natural world that is not contingent on something else? If your answer is no, how did everything get here? Remember, there's no such thing as infinite regression.

Thankfully, the people who think about this stuff for a living have concluded that there must be a source or a *first* non-contingent thing for all contingent objects and events to exist. They call this first thing a *necessary being*. Why is this being called *necessary*? It's pretty simple. For the universe and everything in it to exist, this being *must* exist.

QUESTIONS FOR REFLECTION AND DISCUSSION

- So what or who is this necessary being? Make a list of possible candidates. There's only one condition: The necessary being by definition must be *self-existent, uncaused,* and *eternal.*

Clue #2: CAUSATION—What is the first cause that started all the other causes?

This clue relates closely to Clue #1, but rather than showing how the existence of contingent things requires a necessary being, this clue points to the beginning of the universe as a good reason to believe there must be a cause outside of the universe. Furthermore, because the universe must have a beginning, it must have a cause.

But don't just take our word for it. Here is a classic argument, sometimes called the *kalam* cosmological argument (*kalam* is an Arabic word that means "speech"). Here's how it goes:

1. Whatever begins to exist has a cause.
2. The universe began to exist.
3. Therefore, the universe has a cause.

Now, you may have heard of a scientific theory that says the universe caused itself, but recent astronomical evidence has convinced the vast majority of scientists that the universe was created fifteen billion years ago (give or take a billion years) in a fiery explosion, and that the "seeds" of everything that has happened in the universe since that time were planted in that first instant. And yes, scientists use the word *created*.

Following the kalam argument, there's a big question to explore: Was the "first cause" an impersonal event, like the Big Bang, or a personal agent? Oh, but you're too smart for this question. You've already detected a flaw in the first choice (go ahead, say it: *All events have causes*).

So now you're on to the follow-up question: Is this "personal agent" God? If you're an honest skeptic, that's a tough question. If you already believe that God is real, this is a reasonable conclusion. Tim Keller puts it this way: "The theory that there is a God who made the world accounts for the evidence we see better than the theory that there is no God."[3]

Clue #3: CHARACTER—Why do we have a moral obligation?

We like the way C. S. Lewis approaches this clue, sometimes called the moral argument. He proposes that an "objective law-giver" must exist, not only because we know what is right and wrong, but also because we feel an obligation to do what is right. If this were not the case,

- moral disagreements would make no sense (which they do);
- all criticism of immoral behavior would be meaningless (which it is not);
- it would be unnecessary to keep promises or legal agreements (which we do); and
- we would not make excuses for breaking the objective moral law (which we do).

Based on these observations, Lewis concludes that there must be a moral lawgiver. Societies create laws to manage human behavior, but ultimately we know what is right and wrong even without laws, and we feel an obligation to do right, even when we don't. This moral obligation is commonly referred to as a *conscience*, which begs the question: Where does our conscience come from? Take a look at Romans 2:14–15 for one possible answer:

> Indeed, when Gentiles, who do not have the law, do by nature things required by the law, they are a law for themselves, even though they do not have the law. They show that the requirements of the law are written on their hearts, their consciences also bearing witness, and their thoughts sometimes accusing them and at other times even defending them.

QUESTIONS FOR REFLECTION AND DISCUSSION

- We are suggesting that the answer to these three questions— Why is there something rather than nothing? What is the first cause that started all the other causes? Why do we have a moral obligation?—is God, because only God is self-existent, uncaused, and eternal. Think like an atheist for a minute. What other answer would be as reasonable?
- Which answer requires more faith?

Can You Know God?

If you're not feeling all warm and fuzzy about a God who is self-existent, uncaused, and eternal, we understand. As necessary as these qualities are for God, they seem impersonal. There has to be more to him than mere explanations or descriptions. The good news is that *there is more to God*—much more. But before we move on to some of God's more personal qualities, let's dig deeper into what these three qualities tell us about God.

Because God is self-existent, uncaused, and eternal, he doesn't need anything or anyone. Yet God wants to have a relationship with us, not because he *needs* to, but because he *wants* to. Here's how the apostle Paul explained it to the philosophers of Athens:

> "The God who made the world and everything in it is the Lord of heaven and earth and does not live in temples built by human hands. And he is not served by human hands, as if he needed anything. Rather, he himself gives everyone life and breath and everything else."
>
> Acts 17:24–25

Because God is the *necessary being* and the *first cause* of everything, he is the *beginning* of everything (Genesis 1:1). God didn't need to create the universe, but he did. He didn't need to create humankind, but he did. And he didn't just create a simple universe and one-dimensional human beings. God poured out extravagance, complexity, and variety on his creation on an unimaginable scale. And when it came to his crowning achievement (Genesis 1:26–27), he stamped humanity with his own divine imprint, giving us some of the same qualities he has, making it possible for us to truly relate to him.

This is why we can know God. He isn't some impersonal force or distant being. Because he made us in his image, his personality is familiar. His infinite power and knowledge and his unique ability to be everywhere at once may be way above and beyond us, but we know what it's like to love, to have mercy, to be faithful, honest, and true. We long to have these characteristics consistently and without blemish. That's why we long to know God, who also has these qualities in perfect measure.

A Few Things to Know About God

Here is a series of verses from the Bible that give us a picture of what God is like. This is not an exhaustive list of God's qualities (theologians call them *attributes*), but it's a good place to start. Write out your own description next to each verse or verses, and explain briefly how these help you better know God.

Deuteronomy 32:4

Psalm 139:1–4

Psalm 139:7–12

Psalm 145:8–9

Isaiah 40:28

Luke 18:19

John 17:3

James 1:17

1 Peter 1:15–16

2 Peter 3:8–9

1 John 4:7–9

Revelation 1:8

What Now?

It's important to know that God exists, and it's even more important to know that you can know God. He is not some dependent and impersonal force. He is the independent and personal God whose perfect character fills the universe and brings goodness to our world and our lives. God is generous, creative, loving, faithful, and true—not because he chooses to be, but because he simply is. In other words, God cannot *not* be God. And because he is, we are here, thinking about him, talking about him, and marveling at those qualities that make him God.

To top it off, you can have a personal relationship with this self-existent, uncaused, eternal God who loves you and knows you more completely than anyone else possibly could.

Now that's something to wrestle with.

QUESTIONS FOR REFLECTION AND DISCUSSION

- Were there any attributes of God that surprised you?
- Which ones can you apply personally?
- What is the difference between knowing God exists and knowing God?
- Are both necessary for belief?

2

Why Did God Create Us?

Introduction

Where the three of us live, work, and participate in Christian community, we rarely run across someone who has no understanding of the Christian faith. We know lots of people who don't believe it and plenty of folks (like you and us) who wrestle with their big questions about God and faith, but very few people have absolutely no knowledge of Christian belief or practice. But when we do get to share a conversation with someone who has no preexisting knowledge of Christian belief, it's always an enlightening and challenging (in a good way) conversation. Why? Because people with no biblical or Christian background ask great questions.

A guy who fit this description was introduced to me (Chris) a few months back. After hearing the story of Jesus for the very first time, this guy immediately surrendered his life to Christ. However, prior to that, he had no—absolutely zero—interaction with a Christian church, any doctrines of Christianity, or any people who had self-identified themselves as Christians. Needless to say,

I was eager to delve into conversations with this guy who was an anomaly in the realm of Christian conversion experience.

At one of our coffee meetings, we talked about God's record of his beautiful creation and our sinful fall in the first three chapters of Genesis. When we read the verses in which God punishes Adam and Eve for their sinful rebellion, my new friend closed his Bible, paused for a while, and then said, "Okay. I have a question." I braced myself for a question like this: Why a serpent? Were Adam and Eve real or metaphorical? Did God really have to punish them? But instead, he asked me a question I had never deeply considered before. With a serious and inquisitive tone, he said, "I get why God created the mountains and animals and other beautiful stuff. But why—particularly since we screwed it all up—did he create us?"

That new Christian asked a pretty good question, right? And it's a particularly insightful question in light of those first few chapters in the Bible. In Genesis 1 and 2, we're told that God created all that there is—from the tiniest quark to the ever-expanding cosmos—simply by saying, "Let there be . . ." (This is an underlying doctrine of Christian belief.) Included in this epic start-up was God's most prized creation: humans. Adam and Eve. People. You and us.

But it took all of a few minutes (okay, maybe a bit longer than that) for those first people to give God the cold shoulder (or perhaps it was more like the spiritual equivalent of the finger!). Like rebellious teens, they stood smiling in agreement as the instructions for life were given, but as soon as God the Father turned around, they stuck out their tongues and ran off to do what they wanted. That rebellious spirit, which is in all of us, is what broke—and continues to break—our world.

So if God is all-knowing (which is another orthodox Christian belief), then he knew we would selfishly do our own thing. And if he knew our rebellion would wreak havoc for many millennia to come, why did God bother with the creation of humans in the first place? Why take on the headache? Why create any of us at all?

We Do What We Are

Have you ever taken a personality test? Over the years we've taken several of them: Myers-Briggs, StrengthsFinder, Insights, and even a handful of free personality tests online. In general, the purpose of these tests is to help you discover the ways you are predisposed to think, act, and communicate. Supposedly, this process of self-discovery allows you to achieve greater efficiency, influence, and coordination with others on your team (be that work, family, volunteer organization, etc.). The theory is this: What you do comes out of who you are. Your actions are a direct result of your personality.

For instance, someone who is a strong administrator probably has a natural inclination for organization, problem solving, and work ethic. Someone who thinks strategically is best equipped to see the big picture, while the person who doesn't mind conflict probably thrives as a manager. Or someone who is an artist scores off the charts in creativity and emotional connectedness, while probably not naturally gravitating toward structure or competitiveness.

Have you ever wondered if God is the same way? Could we explain his behavior or at least better understand him by examining his personality traits (theologians prefer the word *attributes,* but whoever heard of an Attributes Assessment Profile)? Is it possible that we could develop a DPA (Divinical Personality Assessment) in order to reveal the reasons why God does what he does (such as create a bunch of humans with a penchant for disobedience)? An in-depth examination of *who* God is might provide insight as to the *why* of what he does. This could prove to be an enlightening undertaking, but the magnitude of the task seems theologically intimidating, because the apostle Paul reminds us that we can never fully understand the complexity of the mind of God (Romans 11:34).

Of course, we wouldn't have to design the DPA (which would take a lot of work) if God simply agreed to complete one of those online Personality Profile Assessment questionnaires. God just needs to log on to one website; that's all we're asking.

Okay, we are getting dangerously close to heresy and/or sacrilege by over-anthropomorphizing God (that is, demeaning him by bringing him down to a human level, when in fact he is the wholly holy Deity). So let's simply opt to consider three character traits of God—*creativity*, *freedom*, and *love*—each of which might help us wrestle with this chapter's big question: Why did God create *us*?

QUESTIONS FOR REFLECTION AND DISCUSSION

- If you were to list some attributes or adjectives that describe God, which ones first come to mind?
- Which ones are biblical?
- Do any of them seem to naturally connect to the question at hand: Why did God create us? If so, which ones and why?

CREATIVITY: Creators Create

So the question as already stated is quite simple: *Why* did God create us? That question presupposes our belief that God designed and built the cosmos and that he created and crafted us to live in it. (If you aren't yet at that point of belief, no worries. Just keep reading.) Instead of beginning our discussion of God's creativity by looking at him as the Creator, let's approach the question from the back door. Let's begin by examining the creation, including all of us human creatures. Thinking about how God has wired us to be a certain way and do particular things might give us insight into God's own nature.

In Genesis 1:26–27 (NLT), the Bible famously concludes the first-chapter creation narrative like this:

> Then God said, "Let us make human beings in our image, to be like us. . . ." So God created human beings in his own image. In the image of God he created them; male and female he created them.

So we were not just created by God, but created in a way that actually reflects God himself. This theological idea is often called the *imago dei*. *Imago dei* is Latin and means "image of God." As beings created in the image of God, we carry God's likeness—not necessarily in physical attributes (because God would be a pasty white guy if he looked like any one of the three of us)—but in our *essence*. We are able to reason and think, self-reflect and emote, communicate and love in ways that none of God's other creations can. And in our male-ness and female-ness, as people designed for relationship in families, communities, friendships, and marriages, we can display an endless array of God's multifaceted image.

One of the ways we reflect his image is in how *we* create. Have you noticed that human beings, unlike the rest of the animal kingdom, are infinitely creative? Walk into a museum, and you will discover that from the beginning of time humans have created amazing and original art. Museums in every culture display the beautiful paintings, sculptures, and handmade antiquities imagined by the human mind and fashioned by human hands.

Or simply walk into a city center and look around. Architects have designed and craftsmen have constructed buildings that touch the sky. Car designers and engineers have envisioned and built driving machines of all shapes and sizes. Pedestrians make their way to lunch, where they will eat any one of a thousand different meals concocted by chefs and sandwich artisans from all over the world. Observe what people are wearing, and you'll see the latest fashion trends conceived by apparel designers. And what are those pedestrians listening to? Creative collaborations of talented musicians and gifted songwriters, or perhaps engaging books written by an imaginative author and recorded by a talented voice artist—either of which is being played on a technologically advanced smartphone.

Doesn't this kind of creative complexity strike you as awesome? But it doesn't stop there. The creativity continues with the fascinating work of entrepreneurs, inventors, scientists, actors, teachers, and their students. Don't these cultural observations suggest that God has gifted humans with an insatiable appetite for creativity? Everything we can observe in the world that rings of imagination and design should give us a clue about why God created us. Connecting the dots—from the created back to the Creator—reveals the metanarrative of God's plan for humanity:

- We are wonderfully and delightfully creative.
- We create because we are human.
- As humans, we bear the image of God, who is remarkable and infinitely creative.
- God created every unique and creative human (not to mention every mountain, flower, animal, planet, star, and particle in the universe).
- God created because he is a Creator.

Without getting entangled in the anthropomorphic trap again, we'll just assume that if God completed an online personality test, creativity would register prominently as a strength.

Could it be that God created humankind, including you and us, because he is, at his core, a creator? And if all creators create, why wouldn't *the* Creator create? And why wouldn't we, as the creative image bearers of God, have a conspicuous role in his grand plan of creation?

God Continues to Create . . . In and Through Us

Deism is the belief that there is a god who created the universe but stepped away, leaving the creation to function on its own. This is not the Christian belief. The Bible and orthodox Christianity teach that God is intimately involved with his creation. He is still sustaining the ongoing cycles and functions of our world (Job 12:10; Isaiah 45:7; 1 Chronicles 29:11; Hebrews 2:8; Proverbs 19:21; Matthew 6:26; 10:29; Romans 8:28). And by the Holy Spirit, we can know him personally and see his involvement in the intimate details of our lives (Psalm 23; 46:1; Joshua 1:9; Matthew 28:20; John 15:1–5; Romans 10:13; Hebrews 13:5). It is there, in the intimate moments of our lives, that we also experience God as a creator.

Jesus' life is the ultimate example of God's interacting creatively and intimately with us through the details of our lives. As God, he created all we know (John 1:1–5), and as God in the flesh, he constantly *re*-created all we know. He re-created lame party drinks into great ones (John 2:1–11 records Jesus' turning tap water into fine wine), and he re-created a boy's snack into a crowd's meal (John 6:1–15 is where Jesus miraculously fed five thousand folks from what was basically just a Happy Meal).

But more importantly and more astoundingly, Jesus re-created one man's limp hand (Matthew 12:9–14), another's blind eyes (John 9), and another's crippled legs (Mark 2:1–12). He re-created a woman's social identity by healing her disease (Mark 5:25–34) and another woman's family by healing her demon-possessed daughter (Matthew 15:21–28). Jesus re-created life when he raised Lazarus from the dead (John 11) and when, after dying a brutal death on the cross for us, he walked out of his own tomb (Mathew 28; Mark 16; Luke 24; John 20), conquering sin and death forever.

Today, Jesus is still at it. By the Holy Spirit, he is re-creating one life at a time that surrenders to him. As Paul wrote, "If anyone is in Christ, he is a new creation. The old has passed away; behold, the new has come" (2 Corinthians 5:17 ESV).

In the future, God will again flex his creative muscles to usher in a new heaven and new earth. The apostle John recorded this prophecy:

> Then I saw "a new heaven and a new earth," for the first heaven and the first earth had passed away. . . . I saw the Holy City, the new Jerusalem, coming down out of heaven from God, prepared as a bride beautifully dressed for her husband. And I heard a loud voice from the throne saying, "Look! God's dwelling place is now among the people, and he will dwell with them. They will be his people, and God himself will be with them and be their God. 'He will wipe every tear from their eyes. There will be no more death' or mourning or crying or pain, for the old order of things has passed away." He who was seated on the throne said, "I am making everything new!" Then he said, "Write this down, for these words are trustworthy and true."
>
> Revelation 21:1–5

QUESTIONS FOR REFLECTION AND DISCUSSION

- What is something you do that stems from who you are?
- Have you ever thought of creation—both the earth and humanity—as a result of God just being God?
- What else about life is an extension of who God is?
- Do you think of God when you or others create new things? Why or why not?

FREEDOM: The Autonomy to Create Us

There is another aspect of God that is worth considering as we wrestle with the reason(s) God created us: his freedom. We are in no way trying to use this characteristic of God as an easy way out, but there is truth to the following statement: God created us simply because he was free to do so.

At first, that simplistic and obvious statement seems to be more of a childish chant than a compelling argument. It's kind of like asking a child why he or she did a particular thing, only to receive the retort: "Because I wanted to." Not helpful. Similarly weak on the persuasive scale is that standard teenage response to an inquiry about questionable behavior: "Well, it's a free country, isn't it?" And don't forget the parental equivalent: "Because I said so."

Our human tendencies aside, the seemingly infantile platitude that "God created us because he was free to do so" actually contains an accurate declaration of a foundational truth that might help us further understand why God bothered to fashion the human race: God *is* completely free.

We aren't the first ones to contemplate the ramifications of God's freedom. At least one other person beat us to the punch by about 2,400 years. It was Aristotle, the influential Greek philosopher from the fourth century BC. He proposed a monotheistic philosophical concept called the "unmoved mover." Aristotle taught that everything had to originate from something that could not be acted upon, or moved. Thus the name "unmoved mover." Aristotle may not have believed in the God of the Old Testament, but his philosophy lined up perfectly with Jewish theology. This unmoved mover is God.

Why It Matters

Does Aristotle's philosophy about God matter? It should, and here's why. If God can be moved by anything else, he is not completely, 100 percent free. And if he is not 100 percent free, he cannot do anything he wants whenever he wants. But if he *is* the unmoved mover, 100 percent free to do as he chooses without being acted upon by any other force, then we should at least consider that he can—and will—do whatever he wants. So perhaps God created us just because he wanted to!

Scripture also bears witness to God's ability to do what he wants. King Nebuchadnezzar, an ancient Babylonian monarch, came face-to-face with the living God. With powerful insight he declared, "He does as he pleases with the powers of heaven and the peoples of the earth. No one can hold back his hand or say to him: 'What have you done?'" (Daniel 4:35).

One of the psalmists knew the same truth and wrote, "Our God is in heaven; he does whatever pleases him" (Psalm 115:3).

Then, in the Bible's final book, the apostle John reports his glimpse of the future worship of God, where the immortal creatures of heaven declare, "You are worthy, O Lord our God, to receive glory and honor and power. For you created all things, and they exist because you created what you pleased" (Revelation 4:11 NLT).

Biblical scholar Stanley Grenz gives helpful insight about the freedom of God as it relates to his creation of us:

> The Creator calls the universe into existence as an act that originates in his own freedom. Because creation is the product of the divine freedom, we may speak of the existence of the world as arising from God's free choice. On the basis of his own prerogative, God chooses to make the world with which to share his own existence. But the choice *for* creation is also a choice *against* the alternative, the decision not to create. Hence, as Karl Barth observed, in creation God chooses "something" and rejects "nothing." God rejects the nothingness of the void. He willfully says "no" to non-existence. Yet even this spurned nothingness ought not be interpreted as a quasi-something with which God does battle and overcomes in creation. Nor ought we to suggest that in creating the world God overcomes his own reluctance. The importance of this is evident from the parallel point: In addition to being a free act, creation is God's loving act.[1]

As Grenz explains, creativity and freedom are part of who God is. Those aspects of God's nature explain, in part, why God spoke humanity into existence. But as Grenz also pointed out, it is God's love that offers the most insight to the question "Why did God create us?" Fittingly, love is the third and final divine attribute we will now examine.

QUESTIONS FOR REFLECTION AND DISCUSSION

- Does the idea that God created us simply because he is God and is free to do so help or hinder your search for why God created us?
- We are imaginative and artistic beings (like God, only to a far lesser degree), but are we as perfectly free as he is? Why or why not?
- How does God's freedom as the "unmoved mover" affect the way you think about him and what he does?

LOVE: The Ultimate Reason for Creation

God is a creator. God is free. And perhaps those characteristics of God played a role in why he chose to bring humanity into existence (even though he knew in advance the horrid consequences of humanity's insurrection). But there is one characteristic of God that the Bible clearly says is primary to his identity: love. Could this characteristic of God be the most significant force behind his will to create us?

"God is love," the apostle John proclaims in 1 John 4:8. The way John describes God, not only is love an important part of who God is, but it *is* who God is. And we see this truth proclaimed throughout all of Scripture. Here's a quick review:

- "The Lord, the Lord, the compassionate and gracious God, slow to anger, abounding in love and faithfulness" is how God personally describes himself to Moses in Exodus 34:6. The truth of this statement so resonates with other biblical writers that they repeat it, in whole and in part, in Numbers 14:18; Nehemiah 9:31; Psalm 86:5, 15; Joel 2:13.

- "Know therefore that the Lord your God is God, the faithful God who keeps covenant and steadfast love with those who love him and keep his commandments, to a thousand generations" (Deuteronomy 7:9 ESV).

- "Oh give thanks to the Lord, for he is good; for his steadfast love endures forever!" (1 Chronicles 16:34 ESV). Passages like these that speak to God's steadfast love are too numerous to list. The Psalms in particular are chock-full of this kind of reference to God's love.

- In John 12, Jesus tells his followers to "love each other as I have loved you" (John 15:12).

- John 3:16 is so famous and quoted so often that we can forget it's actually about an unbelievably loving God! "God so loved the world, that he gave his only Son, that whoever believes in him should not perish but have eternal life" (ESV).

- Even in the middle of our rebellion, his love is overwhelming. Paul wrote, "But God showed his great love for us by sending Christ to die for us while we were still sinners" (Romans 5:8 NLT). In another letter he wrote, "But God, being rich in mercy, because of the great love with which he loved us, even when we were dead in our trespasses, made us alive together with Christ" (Ephesians 2:4–5 ESV).

The Bible says God is love, and it also teaches that love begets more love. (Please excuse the archaic "begets" terminology, but it sounds so biblical if read out loud.) In more contemporary language, love produces more love. Because Christ loved us first, our natural response is to love him in return (1 John 4:19). And because of the transforming love of Christ within us, we can love other Christians (John 13:35), and we can love our neighbors to the same degree that we love ourselves (Mark 12:31).

Like a giant magnet, love is attractive. And it's contagious. When people love one another, others want to experience it. Love is life-producing, life-giving, regenerative, and multiplying. When a man and woman are deeply rooted in a self-giving, loving marriage, the unconditional love of their children is a natural by-product. When you love what you do, what you eat, what you watch, and what you experience—you want to do it, eat it, watch it, and experience it more, and you want others to do the same. Why? Because love multiplies.

Grenz continues his perspective on God's creative love with a strong statement: "The basis of the act of creation lies solely in God's love."[2] Yet God does not love because he needs to complete himself by creating an object for his affection; nor did God create humans because he was needy for love from them; nor did he need to prove his power or awesomeness by showing off and creating creatures in his image. "God's love," Grenz writes, "is already complete within the Trinity apart from the act of creation. . . . Because God is the trinitarian community of love, God need not create the world to actualize his character. Yet because God is love his creation of the world is fully in keeping with his character."[3]

It is beyond the scope of this chapter to wrestle with the idea of the Trinity. But not to worry—we will tackle it together in chapter 9. For now, here's something to consider: If God the Father, Son, and Holy Spirit have always existed in a perfect, loving, three-persons-in-one community, doesn't it make sense that God would create us to love and be loved? If God is infinitely more loving, giving, and caring than we are, why would he not also enjoy seeing that love multiply into an amazing universe and a lot of image-bearing people? "Because God is love," Grenz writes, "God is self-giving. Because God is self-giving, God willingly creates the world."[4]

Why did God create us? Why not? And if God truly is love, why not share the wealth, lavish it on something new, and create beings with the capacity to receive that love and pass it on to others?

Pleased to Create

In the "Why It Matters" section above, we listed three Bible passages. One was from Daniel 4, another from Psalm 115, and the last from Revelation 4. Did you notice which word was used in all three verses? The word that caught our attention was *please*.

- "Our God is in heaven; he does whatever pleases him" (Psalm 115:3).
- "He does all he pleases . . ." (Daniel 4:35).
- " . . . you created what you pleased" (Revelation 4:11).

These verses were originally written in ancient Hebrew (Old Testament) and ancient Greek (New Testament). There are slight variations of meaning for the English verb *to please*. In the Daniel and Revelation verses, *to please* means to do as you will. So God does all he wills, or creates what he wills. This is the freedom and creative part of God. But Psalm 115 is different. In this verse, the original Hebrew word means to take delight in or to bend down. The psalmist is trying to help us see that the God of the universe does nothing out of obligation or uncertainty. He intentionally moves (bends down) and does (creates) what he delights in.

The driving force behind God's creation was his desire to do what pleased him. A God who is creative, free, and loving created a people designed to be creative, free, and loving. And he takes great delight in what he has done.

QUESTIONS FOR REFLECTION AND DISCUSSION

- After working through this chapter, how has your view of God changed?

- How has your view of yourself as someone created by God changed?

- Imagine having a discussion with someone who views God as a vengeful, implacable deity who couldn't care less about humans. What would you say to this person?

3

Why Doesn't God Make Himself More Obvious?

Introduction

It was Easter Sunday, and I (Chris) was roaming our church patio welcoming those who were arriving for the service. After the last few families shuffled in, I saw a guy in his late twenties sitting alone at a patio table, earphones in, watching a video on his phone. I walked toward him and decided to say something if he lifted his eyes to meet mine—though he looked completely disinterested in what was going on around him.

He made eye contact with me as I approached him, so I introduced myself. "My name is Jacob," he said in response. Perhaps thinking that I was going to invite him to come into the auditorium for the Easter celebration, he continued, "I hope you're not offended, but I don't get this whole God thing."

If that wasn't an open invitation to sit down and talk honestly with him about spiritual matters—especially on the most sacred of days—I don't know what was. So I accepted. Jacob told me his mom was inside, and that she longed for him to join her in the service. But he would go no closer than the patio. And he was ready to tell me why.

"God has never made himself obvious to me," he said with some regret in his voice. "I've asked. I've prayed many times for God—if he's out there—to prove it to me. Why doesn't he show up? Why doesn't he do something to prove to me that he's real?"

For the next hour I listened as Jacob shared some of his story, including a deep desire for God to reveal himself, to tell Jacob whether or not to marry his girlfriend, and to convince him that gathering at an organized church is something God actually wants.

When the conversation was over, I couldn't help but think that Jacob's core question was a very good one. Even more, it was a question I've asked myself many times: "Why doesn't God make himself more obvious?"

■ ▓ ■

One of the greatest obstacles to people knowing God is his hiddenness. Think about it. If you wanted to build a meaningful relationship with someone and they constantly played hard to get—or even more, hard to find—that would be just a little frustrating. And it would be a surefire way to end things before they even started.

Now imagine that the person who was hard to find was also invisible. Talk about a relationship killer! But doesn't that seem like God's style sometimes? Doesn't he seem to go mute at the precise time we are asking him to speak to us? And what's up with his invisibility? Does he really think that his invisibility gives us confidence in his existence?

Suddenly Jacob, the patio-bound skeptic, doesn't seem so stubborn. He's just admitting what everyone else thinks, only he refuses even to enter God's house until God makes it obvious that he's there.

QUESTIONS FOR REFLECTION AND DISCUSSION

- Do Jacob's questions and frustrations resonate with you?
- When have you been annoyed by God's apparent absence?
- On the flip side, have you ever experienced God in an undeniably tangible way?
- What do you feel when you read a story in the Bible about someone who saw, heard, or touched God, Jesus, or the Holy Spirit in some way?
- Are there other things in life that aren't obvious and perhaps even invisible? What do you do with those?

God and the Obvious

What do we mean when we ask the question, "Why doesn't God make himself more obvious?" Do we want God to be so constantly obvious that he becomes ordinary? Should God-sightings be commonplace and routine? And should he be blatantly obvious to everyone in the same way?

Do we want God to be like the answer to a puzzle? Does a puzzle's obviousness make it more valuable? Or is the opposite true: The harder something is to solve, the more rewarding the result?

Would diamonds be more or less valuable if they were commonplace and easy to extract? Would gold be worth more if it were as common as dust? Would pearls be more prized if they were . . . you get the idea. The things with the most value are often the most hidden and least obvious.

Let's get more personal. Which of the human emotions carries the highest value? Gratitude? Affection? Sympathy? As positive and beneficial as those emotions are, they arise with relative frequency. They occur often enough that we've grown accustomed to them. Their expression may elicit momentary appreciation, but it won't merit mention in your daily journal. By contrast, the emotion of love, *true love* (thank you, *Princess Bride*), is much more elusive. For many, it is the object of a lifelong search. True love is valued, in part, because it is universally acknowledged to be such a rare treasure.

So it is with God. As we discovered in the last chapter, we can quite easily compare him with love because he is love (1 John 4:8). When others judge and condemn us, God says, "I love you." Yet that love—like God—is sometimes hidden. We don't always *feel* as though God loves us. In fact, if we were being completely honest (and that's the goal here), we may rarely or never feel God's love. But that doesn't mean it's not there. And we may carry some of the responsibility for that. Maybe we're not in a position to evaluate God's love for what it's worth. Or even more importantly, we may not know God well enough to understand the nature of his love. We may be receiving it, but not realizing it because we don't understand him.

QUESTIONS FOR REFLECTION AND DISCUSSION

- What would happen if God made himself obvious to everyone?
- What if he were obvious to you all the time? Would you welcome that, or would you have a different response?
- Why is it that we treasure the things in life that are more rare?

What Is God Really Like?

In order to wrestle with the hiddenness of God, we need to venture into an area most people fear to tread: theology. Don't be misled by the urban myth that theology is ponderous and ill-suited for the faint of heart. Theology is simply the study of the nature of God, and believe it or not, you're already doing it. And with an inquisitive mind and a willing heart, you are adequately equipped for this diversion.

One of the goals of theology is to uncover and explain God's characteristics, or attributes. These attributes help us answer questions such as, "What is God like?" and "How does he relate to the universe and everything in it?" When it comes to God's hiddenness, we think there are three attributes that help us understand why this is often the case:

- God is a Spirit (John 1:18).
- God is invisible (John 1:18).
- God is eternal (1 Timothy 1:17).

God Is an Invisible Spirit and Present Everywhere at the Same Time

From a human perspective, an invisible deity can be frustrating, but for God, invisibility has definite advantages. A physical (and therefore visible) God would be restricted. He could be in only one place at a time. But being a form-free Spirit, God is unrestricted by space and time. He is not bound by the physical laws that restrict us mere mortals.

Another one of God's characteristics is that he is everywhere at one time (the theological term is *omnipresent*). King David, who wrote many of the Psalms in the Bible, expressed God's omnipresence using poetic language that can stir your soul:

> Where shall I go from your Spirit?
>   Or where shall I flee from your presence?
> If I ascend to heaven, you are there!
>   If I make my bed in Sheol, you are there!
> If I take the wings of the morning
>   and dwell in the uttermost parts of the sea,
> even there your hand shall lead me,
>   and your right hand shall hold me.
>   Psalm 139:7–10 ESV

Here's the beautiful thing about this quality of God. He is present to you while at the same time present to others in your family, your circle of friends, indeed, the whole world. When you feel God's presence in your life, it's very personal. Yet anyone else can sense that same presence at the same time. That's the essence of omnipresence, and it would not be possible if God were not invisible.

God Is Eternal and Infinite

Here's another quality that complements the invisibility and omnipresence of God: He is eternal. That means he has no beginning and no end. God exists outside of time by virtue of his eternal nature. Just as you have the opportunity to know God and experience his love, mercy, and forgiveness, so did your ancestors, and so will your descendants. There's a saying, "God has no grandchildren," which is a truth made possible by virtue of God's eternal nature. Every person in every generation has the privilege of being God's own adopted son or daughter.

In addition to God's invisibility, omnipresence, and eternal nature, there's another attribute to consider: God is infinite. On a theological level, that means everything about God—his love, grace, and power—is without boundary. What that means to you personally is immensely important. As a child of God, your needs will never outrun God's infinite supply.

We are more accustomed to human attributes, so it is natural that we might prefer a God who is more like us, more . . . well, natural. But if God divested himself of the supernatural attributes, we'd have a God who is more obvious but less effectual. If God were visible rather than hidden, tangible and physical rather than everywhere-at-once, and bound by time rather than being eternal, he would be less than God, which would make him not God at all. And he would be of far less benefit to you.

QUESTIONS FOR REFLECTION AND DISCUSSION

- What are the benefits to you personally of a God who is Spirit?
- How does his invisibility help you?
- What is the difference between God's being eternal and infinite?
- Do these qualities make God more or less accessible to you?

Hiding in Plain Sight

Now, back to the specific issue of God's hiddenness. Maybe we are mistaken if we think God is hiding. Just because God is invisible doesn't mean we can't see him. God may not be physical, but it is still possible for him to reveal his existence. Theologian Wayne Grudem puts it this way:

> God's invisibility means that God's total essence, all of his spiritual being, will never be able to be seen by us, yet God still shows himself to us through visible, created things.[1]

As it turns out, God has been rather intentional about making himself known, despite the invisibility thing, in two distinct ways: through general revelation and through special revelation (as in "revealing" his presence):

- *God's general revelation:* This refers to the evidence of God's existence that can be seen in the physical world. Consider the magnitude and wonder of the cosmos. And don't forget the intricate functioning of the human body. Psalm 19:1 describes God's general revelation this way:

  > The heavens declare the glory of God;
  >   the skies proclaim the work of his hands.

  Maybe the universe (and all that it contains) is the "obviousness" of God that we have desired to see but are often too preoccupied to notice.

- *God's special revelation:* This is the term that includes the miraculous ways in which God reveals himself. (Creation of the universe was certainly a miracle, but this category includes more specific and isolated revelations.) Special revelation encompasses what people would consider supernatural phenomena, such as physical appearances of God (like when Moses speaks with God at the burning bush in Exodus 3),

God-prompted visions and dreams to the Old Testament prophets, and God-inspired guidance to the authors of Scripture. And then there is the most spectacular special revelation of all: Jesus, the Son of God, coming to earth in human form, performing miracles among the people, and resurrecting the dead back to life, including himself. Hebrews 1:1–2 describes it well:

> In the past God spoke to our ancestors through the prophets at many times and in various ways, but in these last days he has spoken to us by his Son.

God intended that Jesus would be the ultimate "special revelation" of God's own existence.

God is not visible, but neither is he hiding. Through his general and special revelation, he is making it possible for us to find him. This is no game of celestial hide-and-seek. God wants to be found:

> You will seek me and find me when you seek me with all your heart.
>
> Jeremiah 29:13

QUESTIONS FOR REFLECTION AND DISCUSSION

- Here are some verses to stimulate your thinking about God's general revelation: Romans 1:20; 2:15; Psalm 19:1–4. What in this world points to God? What are those things that are most convincing to you?

- What are the things in this world that others believe point to God, but you aren't convinced they do?

- Next, read these verses that speak to God's special revelation: Genesis 41:1–32; Exodus 3:1–4; 2 Timothy 3:16–17; Philippians 2:6–8. Does God's special revelation change your opinion of whether God is hiding or obvious?

- Is the special revelation of Jesus sufficient for you to consider that God has revealed himself to you?

When Seeing Isn't Believing

The apostle Paul (who wrote most of those letters in the New Testament) and the writers of the Psalms (like David) believed that God *has* made himself obvious. These Bible authors would say, "If you want to see God, just look around!" But Scripture is also quite clear that just because God makes himself obvious doesn't mean people will believe.

If the examples we're about to cite to you are any indication, there's no guarantee that our friend Jacob would suddenly yank out his earbuds and stand at attention—even if God were to show up on the church patio like the Fantastic Four's Human Torch.

- God sent a series of plagues on ancient Egypt that were miraculous and quite visible, yet Pharaoh and the Egyptians did not believe (Exodus 4:4–9).

- An entire generation of Israelites witnessed miracles on a daily basis (pillar of fire by night and a cloud by day), but their unbelief prevented them from entering the Promised Land (Numbers 14:26–38).

- Jesus fed 4,000 people by miraculously multiplying seven small loaves and several fish. Afterward, the Pharisees were not impressed and asked for another miracle to prove that Jesus was from God (Mark 8:1–12).

- During his three years of public ministry, Jesus (1) restored sight to the blind, (2) healed diseases, (3) used only five small loaves and two fish to feed more than 5,000 people at one sitting, and—as if those weren't enough—(4) *raised the dead* back to life. Kind of a big deal. Many believed in Jesus after witnessing these things that no mere mortal could do. Even so, many other people witnessed the same events and still refused to believe that Jesus was God (John 12:37).

So in the case of God and Jesus, the actual "seeing" doesn't always lead to believing.

> ### QUESTIONS FOR REFLECTION AND DISCUSSION
> - Have you ever witnessed a miracle?
> - If God did something miraculous and obvious today, do you think you would recognize his work? Would you feel comfortable giving him credit for it? Why or why not?
> - What is your response when others claim God has revealed himself to them?
> - Do you ever question someone else's claim that they witnessed a miracle? If so, does your skepticism arise from a disbelief in God, from suspicion of the legitimacy of miracles, or from a distrust of people's perception of the supernatural?

Why We Can't See God

We need to pause here for a minute and make an assumption about your experience with God to this point in your life. Even though you may be convinced God is real, and even though you may believe God has revealed himself in specific ways, are there times in your life when God nonetheless feels distant and hidden? It's okay to admit it. King David was being very honest when he wrote,

> How long, Lord? Will you forget me forever?
> How long will you hide your face from me?
> Psalm 13:1

The same person who wrote this Psalm also wrote Psalm 19, which declares God is abundantly evident to even a casual observer of the natural world. How can that contrast be reconciled? Why did David declare God's glory after observing the physical world around him (in Psalm 19), only to feel as though God had forgotten him in Psalm 13? Why did David wax poetic in one Psalm about God being everywhere, but in the other express with despair that God was hiding from him? If we assume that God was there all along, then David must have suffered from a type of spasmodic spiritual myopia. There were times in his life when he felt that he couldn't see

God, even though he believed that God was real and present. Faulty spiritual vision is an affliction that infects all of us from time to time.

There are several possible reasons why we lose sight (and a sense) of God:

- *We take general revelation for granted.* Our consciousness becomes callous to God's creation; over a lifetime, the miraculous seems commonplace, and we forget to notice that the wonder of the natural world reveals God. And sadly, sometimes we don't know enough about how the natural world works to realize that there is something or someone supernatural behind it.

- *We're using only our eyes.* Jesus confronted a woman at a well who was struggling to believe. He told her, "God is spirit, and those who worship him must worship in spirit and truth" (John 4:24 ESV). This woman recognized that Jesus, who was standing in front of her, was a prophet, but that wasn't enough. It still isn't. The Bible says this about Jesus: "He is the image of the invisible God" (Colossians 1:15 ESV). Jesus said as much to the woman at the well when she confessed she was looking for the true Messiah: "I who speak to you am he" (John 4:26). The woman was looking only with her eyes, when she should have been seeing Jesus by faith.

- *We're not trained to see God.* We must be taught the things of God, and we must be shown how to relate to him (Deuteronomy 6:4ff; 1 Samuel 3:1ff; Proverbs 22:6; Matthew 28:19–20; 1 Timothy 4:15–16). Some of us were raised in churches that taught us to sing, read the Bible, and be moral people. But they never taught us to actually look for and experience God. Others of us have no church background and were conditioned to look for completely different things than God.

- *We have short-term memories.* There is a reason why God repeatedly told the people of Israel to *remember* what he had done for them (Exodus 13:3; Deuteronomy 5:15; 7:18;

15:15; 24:18; 1 Chronicles 16:12ff; Psalm 105:5; 143:5; and many more through the prophets). They had a tendency to forget. So do we.

- *We're not looking very hard.* If we're honest, we have to admit that we want God to do all the work in this relationship. We want *him* to show up, to pursue us, and to reveal himself. We put the burden on him to make an effort and take some initiative, yet we don't require the same of ourselves. James wrote it simply and poignantly: "Come near to God and he will come near to you" (James 4:8).

- *We're expecting God to provide something that he's not intending to deliver.* We have set expectations for God that he never promised. We anticipate that God will do what we want (never considering that what we desire may be outside of his best plans for us). When God doesn't perform on cue like a trained circus monkey, we default to the "God is distant" conclusion.

- *We don't actually want to see him.* Isn't it true that we have an unspoken fear that if God would make himself obvious to us, we would then have to make some drastic changes in our lives? We're not always ready for that. It is easier to downplay our attempts to communicate with God.

- *We doubt God is real.* Why would God show himself to someone who didn't really believe he existed?

All too often we can't see God because we are getting in the way.

QUESTIONS FOR REFLECTION AND DISCUSSION

- Be honest like David in Psalm 13:1. Write two sentences that express your frustration that God has sometimes hidden from you.
- Rank the eight possible reasons why you lose sight of God, with the first being the most common reason and the eighth being the least common.
- Looking at your list, what can you do to shorten this list?

Sometimes God Hides on Purpose

In all of the above-listed reasons, we presumed that God is ever-present, but it is we who are obscuring our own ability to see and sense God. That's a good assumption for most of us, most of the time. But there's another aspect to this whole divine hiddenness thing. Is it possible that sometimes God clothes himself in camouflage on purpose, intentionally making it difficult for us to find him?

Our friend Mike Erre has written a fascinating book called *Astonished: Recapturing the Wonder, Awe, and Mystery of Life With God*. We like that title because it states very simply how much we miss when we try to reduce God to something we can easily detect and quickly define. Even more, we think Mike hits the mark when he calls God "wild" and our faith an "adventure."

Mike devotes two chapters in *Astonished* to the "hiddenness" of God. In a stroke of brilliant insight, he makes the case that God sometimes hides from us *on purpose*. In other words, it might not always be our fault if we can't see God. Sometimes he hides from us on purpose. See what you think of these examples of God deliberately hiding from us:[2]

- *God hides from us so that we can hide from him.* The biggest roadblock preventing us from experiencing God's presence in our lives is sin. The prophet Isaiah makes it clear that our sin separates us from God (Isaiah 59:2). It destroys our *intimacy* with God (but not our position as children of God). God is holy and cannot dwell in the presence of sin. He is quick to forgive (1 John 1:9), but those who continue to sin without asking forgiveness run the risk of losing touch with God because of their sin.

- *God may hide information from us because the timing is not right for him to tell us what we want to know.* The most vivid example of this principle concerns the coming of Jesus Christ to the world. In Galatians 4:4 Paul says, "But when the right time came, God sent his Son, born of a woman, subject to the law" (NLT). Before that time, God withheld information concerning the exact time his Son would be born. There were clues, but God hid much of the information concerning what the Messiah would do when he came. The same principle applies to all of us. We would love for God to tell us what is going to happen each day. We get frustrated when we don't know God's will all at once. But God knows better. He gives us just enough light for today, but rarely enough so we can see into the future. Even the Scriptures are described as a "lamp" for our feet, giving us just enough light for the next step rather than a searchlight that illuminates everything ahead of us.

- *God may stay hidden until we honestly seek him.* You wouldn't introduce yourself to someone who isn't interested in knowing you, right? Well, God is a perfect gentleman of sorts, and he won't usually force an encounter. He may prefer to wait until we desire to have a relationship with him. Here's what the book of Hebrews says about those who seek him: "Anyone who wants to come to him must believe that God exists and that he rewards those who sincerely seek him" (Hebrews 11:6 NLT).

QUESTIONS FOR REFLECTION AND DISCUSSION

- What is your reaction to these three examples of God hiding from us?
- Which one do you most identify with?
- Is there an example that troubles you?

Ways We Can Start to Seek and See God

There are some practical ways we can begin (or begin again) to recognize God and to discover for ourselves just how much he wants to be found.

- *Take a walk outside.* If Psalm 19 and Romans 1 are true, taking a walk outside might just help us to see how obvious God has made himself.

- *Stop using our eyes.* If God is spirit—if he is personally invisible to the human eye—then maybe we should stop looking for him just with our eyes.

- *Look in the right places.* God is not restricted to churches or epic hikes in the mountains or private prayer closets. That being said, it might do us well to frequent those places where God seems to show up most often (hint: As Jesus said in Matthew 18:20, wherever a community of believers gathers, God is there).

- *Learn from someone who sees God all the time.* The Bible is full of examples: Samuel had Eli, Ruth had Naomi, and Timothy had Paul to help them see God. The same thing is true for us today. We need mentors, people of the faith who are ahead of us in spiritual maturity, to help us better understand and know God.

- *Take better notes of the time God has revealed himself to you.* Begin recording the times God was obvious to you—answered prayer, miracles, his creation, deep joy, abiding peace when you're going through tough times—so you can refer to them in the future when God doesn't seem obvious and close.

- *Do what you already know to do.* Obedience to God leads to experiencing God (John 14:23).

- *Believe it's possible.* Jesus reminded Thomas in John 20:29, "Blessed are those who have not seen and yet have believed." Most of us do not believe until we see proof. But belief is not the proof. It is the door through which we gain access to the proof. Most of us want to understand before we believe. In fact, as Saint Anselm famously said, we need to believe so that we may understand. And if you've never heard of Saint Anselm, that's okay. The song "Walk On" by U2 says the same thing when it describes "a place that has to be believed to be seen."

Let's Get Personal

Before we conclude this discussion of finding God, we'd like to give you a real-life example of two young married couples, both of similar ages, both successful, both terrific people to be around. Yet there is a big difference in the way they approach their spiritual lives.

The husband and wife in the first couple are both very new in their faith journey. They don't have a lot of knowledge about God, but they are eager to know more. They are involved in the small group ministry at church, and they ask questions about God (similar to the questions we're asking in this book). They still have that sense of wonder that comes from those who are experiencing God for the first time. God isn't always obvious, but to people like them, God is always interesting.

The husband and the wife in the other couple are both long-time Christians. In fact, they graduated from well-known Christian colleges and are very familiar with Christian belief and theology. However, they gather with other Christians infrequently and don't seem all that interested in learning more about their faith. They don't ask questions about God, nor do they discuss the spiritual dynamics of life. Any sense of wonder they have in their lives is directly tied to their own successful careers.

At the risk of generalizing the spiritual personalities of these two couples, it seems to us that the less spiritually "mature" couple shows more enthusiasm for God than does the more mature couple. To put it another way, couple #1 is energized by their faith and eagerly wants to know more about God. By comparison, couple #2 is spiritually content, if not complacent. They know quite a bit about God already, so taking time to know him better isn't a priority. After all, they're busy people!

So who do you think struggles more often with the hiddenness of God? Which couple delights when God shows up in unexpected ways?

We're not saying that if you don't hang out with other believers and don't ask a lot of questions about God, he's going to hide himself from you. Some of the most seasoned Christians we know have struggled with spiritual dryness when God seems as distant as the planet Pluto (or the star Pluto or whatever Pluto is now). We've been through those desert experiences ourselves. But we can tell you that those who seek God sincerely and take God seriously are better equipped to endure those times when God hides. And more often than not, when they cry out to God in times of distress, he answers.

Here's what David writes in Psalm 34:4–7:

> I sought the Lord, and he answered me;
>> he delivered me from all my fears.
> Those who look to him are radiant;
>> their faces are never covered with shame.
> This poor man called, and the Lord heard him;
>> he saved him out of all his troubles.
> The angel of the Lord encamps around those who fear him,
>> and he delivers them.

QUESTIONS FOR REFLECTION AND DISCUSSION

- Do you identify more with couple #1 or couple #2?
- Here's a more direct question: How intentional have you been when it comes to seeking and seeing God?
- What has kept you from putting more effort into your relationship with him?
- Are you afraid of being disappointed? Or have you just been too busy? Both responses are legitimate and nothing to be ashamed of, so take some time to sort this out on your own or with your study group.

4

Can I Trust What the Bible Says About God?

Introduction

Have you ever been involved in a case of mistaken identity, where someone believed (or wanted to believe) that you were someone you were not? I (Chris) experienced this recently in a most unlikely place.

I was doing some shopping at Target, and I happened to be wearing a red shirt (not a good idea in Target). More than once someone asked me for help. The red shirt I was wearing made them think I was a helpful Target team member. As I was picking out some toilet paper, a woman turned the corner, walked down the aisle toward me, and said with a smile, "Excuse me, do you know where the baby wipes are?" I smiled back and said, "I'm sorry, but I don't work here." Either she didn't hear me, or she didn't believe me, because she repeated the question, only this time her smile was replaced with a look of determination: "The baby wipes. Can you tell me which aisle they are on?"

I attempted to clear up the misunderstanding: "I'm sorry, ma'am, but I really don't work here. I guess it's the red shirt." That did not make her happy. She grumbled, "Fine," and turned to find them on her own.

No matter how badly she wanted me to be a Target employee with directions to her desperately needed wipes, it didn't make it true. But her mind was made up. I was a Target employee whether I liked it or not. She probably filed a complaint with management. Hopefully some other guy matching my description didn't get fired.

This story may seem out of place in this chapter about the Bible and its trustworthiness, but it's actually a great illustration for the way people see the world's best-known and best-selling book.

◾ ◼ ◾

Like all best sellers, the Bible has its fans. But there are also critics for whom the Bible is an easy target (see, we told you the opening illustration was relevant). It is estimated that more than six billion Bibles have been printed since Gutenberg printed the first one (in Latin) more than 560 years ago. But that's not what makes the Bible controversial. As we will discuss later, the Bible makes extraordinary claims, but even those aren't what seem to inflame the detractors. Most often, people who are upset with the Bible want it to be an answer book for their questions or a solution to their problems. They want it to be magical, and when it doesn't deliver in that manner, they turn away in a huff to resume their search for answers elsewhere.

What Do You Think of the Bible?

With the Bible, it is not always either/or, where you hate it or you love it. There are a lot of people in the middle who could be described as indifferent or lukewarm toward the Bible. Wherever you are on the spectrum, you could probably give your opinion of the Bible in one or two words. Here are some of the descriptors that we hear most often when we ask, "What do you think of the Bible?": accurate, amazing, bigoted, confusing, contradictory, fairy tale, hard to understand, life changing, miraculous, misogynistic, true story, and trustworthy.

QUESTIONS FOR REFLECTION AND DISCUSSION

- How do you describe the Bible? Do any of the descriptions we've listed match yours?
- What role, if any, did the Bible play in your life when you were growing up?
- What does the Bible do for you now? Does it live up to your expectations, or are there times when you are disappointed with what you read?
- Have there been times when the Bible has been a guide and an inspiration?
- Do you find Bible reading to be a challenge or boring, or maybe even a waste of time? If so, what makes it that way?

If you are still formulating your opinions about the Bible, we suggest that it may be most appropriate and productive for you to ask the question we use for the title of this chapter: Can I trust what the Bible says about God?

This is a threshold question, because so much of what we know about God comes from the Bible.

- *All of those attributes of God we talked about in chapter 3?* We know about them from the Bible.
- *The origin of the universe?* While it's not stated in scientific terminology, the framework for the creation story is found in the Bible (Genesis 1–2).
- *God's rescue plan for the human race?* The most definitive verse is John 3:16.

- *God's secret to the meaning of life and to obtaining the best life ever?* It's revealed throughout the Bible in the form of history, poetry, wisdom, prophecy, and teaching (2 Timothy 3:16; Hebrews 4:12).
- *God's plan for the end of the world and the beginning of heaven?* Go to the back of the Bible and read Revelation 21:1–5, which concludes with this dramatic statement straight from God: *"Write this down, for these words are trustworthy and true."*

Biblical trustworthiness is an imperative for belief in the Bible. If we can't trust the Bible, then we can't trust what it says about God. And that would be a problem.

The trustworthiness of the Bible is relevant not only for what we know about God, but also for what we know about Jesus. As we discussed in chapter 3, *general* revelation (the world around us) provides clues about the Creator's nature, but only the Bible gives us details about God and insights into the way he works in the world. Likewise, the Bible is the sole source for almost everything we know about Jesus. Extra-biblical sources confirm that he lived in first-century Palestine, but only the Bible tells us what he said, and only the Bible shows us what he did, including the miracles he performed to illustrate his authority. If the Bible isn't trustworthy, then what we think we know about Christ is questionable.

The Jefferson Bible: More an Issue of Personal Opinion Than Trustworthiness

Let's get back to opinions for a final moment. As we embark on analyzing the Bible from a reliability perspective, we'll need to remember that the objections of many people to biblical content has nothing to do with issues of reliability of the Bible; they just don't like something the Bible says. Their objections are merely a matter of personal belief, with no substantiation of defect or inaccuracy in Scripture. If they don't believe in miracles, for example, then they object to the Bible because it speaks of miracles, but their objection doesn't mean that the miracles didn't in fact occur. They will gladly accept Jesus as a great moral teacher, but they will try to discredit or ignore the Bible's description of him as a supernatural being who was born of a virgin and rose from the dead. They make no legitimate challenge to the Bible's accuracy other than their lack of belief in the content.

The most notorious example of someone who felt strongly about removing those pesky miracles was one of America's most famous leaders, Thomas Jefferson. The Jefferson Bible, or *The Life and Morals of Jesus of Nazareth* as it is formally titled, was an abridged version of the Gospels from the Bible, compiled by Jefferson in the latter years of his life. He used a razor to cut and paste the sections from the four Gospels that emphasized the teachings of Jesus, while leaving out the miracles of Jesus and any mention of the supernatural, also excluding sections describing the resurrection and other miracles and passages declaring the divinity of Jesus.

Few people would go to the painstaking work that Jefferson did, but there are plenty of people who would agree with Jefferson that parts of the Bible are worth keeping while other parts should be cut, clipped, and trashed. They don't find the Bible to be unreliable and then question the deity of Christ and everything else. It is just the other way around: They abhor the concept that Jesus is God, so they object to those passages about him and yet find the remainder to be acceptable. For example, the renowned atheist Richard Dawkins believes the Bible should be taught because it has had such an impact on our culture. Of course, he wants it taught as fiction, not truth.

Thankfully, the trustworthiness of the Bible does not depend on the personal preferences of Thomas Jefferson or Richard Dawkins. However, if the Word of God is reliable and trustworthy, we may want to set aside our own personal preferences and align ourselves with its teachings.

- In your experience reading the Bible, which part(s) would you cut out to make your own version if you could?
- How would you explain the Bible to someone who's never read it?
- Is it useful to read the Bible simply as an instructional book?
- What's wrong with ignoring its supernatural aspects?
- If you find a portion of the Bible to be objectionable, does that mean that the Bible is unreliable?
- Is trustworthiness dependent upon a reader's assent to everything that he or she reads?

The Bible on the Bible

When reading a book of any kind, we pay attention when the author makes certain claims about the work. For example, the author may say, "This is a true story," or "This is a work of fiction." Those are two very different claims. If it's a work of fiction, then you enjoy it for what it is. If the author says the book is true, there are ways to verify the facts, but you at least start with the truth claim made by the author or authors.

So what does the Bible say about itself? Here are some statements by six authors who wrote books in the Bible:

- "The statutes you have laid down are righteous; they are fully trustworthy" (Psalm 119:138).
- "This is what I told you while I was still with you: Everything must be fulfilled that is written about me in the Law of Moses, the Prophets and the Psalms" (Jesus, recorded by Luke in Luke 24:44).
- "But these are written that you may believe that Jesus is the Messiah, the Son of God, and that by believing you may have life in his name" (the apostle John in John 20:31).
- "All Scripture is God-breathed and is useful for teaching, rebuking, correcting and training in righteousness, so that

72

the servant of God may be thoroughly equipped for every good work" (the apostle Paul, 2 Timothy 3:16–17).

- "For the word of God is alive and active. Sharper than any double-edged sword, it penetrates even to dividing soul and spirit, joints and marrow; it judges the thoughts and attitudes of the heart" (Hebrews 4:12).

- "For we did not follow cleverly devised stories when we told you about the coming of our Lord Jesus Christ in power, but we were eyewitnesses of his majesty" (the apostle Peter in 2 Peter 1:16).

- "Above all, you must understand that no prophecy of Scripture came about by the prophet's own interpretation of things. For prophecy never had its origin in the human will, but prophets, though human, spoke from God as they were carried along by the Holy Spirit" (2 Peter 1:20–21).

Thomas Jefferson wanted the Bible and Jesus to be something they were not. But no matter how deep his desire was for the Bible to be just a book of moral teachings, and Jesus to simply be a good teacher, the Bible and Jesus claim much more than that.

QUESTIONS FOR REFLECTION AND DISCUSSION

- After reading these passages of Scripture, how would you explain what the Bible says about itself?
- How does understanding what the Bible claims about itself help you wrestle with its trustworthiness?

Who Wrote the Bible?

We quoted from six Bible authors, but there are thirty-four others who collectively wrote the sixty-six books of the Bible over a 1,600-year period—from 1500 BC, when Moses wrote the first five books of the Bible, to around AD 100, when John wrote the book of Revelation.

So who were these guys? Well, for one thing, they were human. When you think about it, that in itself is astounding. God used ordinary human beings to write a history of the human race, from creation through the life, death, and resurrection of Jesus, and covering the beginnings of his worldwide church. God used these people who weren't all that different from you and us (except they probably had more hair but fewer hair products) to describe his plan to rescue the planet and its inhabitants from the consequences of their rebellion.

Forty authors writing the Bible! Sounds like a bit of a free-for-all, doesn't it? This fact alone may make you question the reliability of the Bible. But wait, it gets worse. Except for maybe one or two part-time poets in the gang, not one of these authors was a full-time writer. Not a single one was a professional journalist, trained in fact-finding and reporting. There were a few who were highly educated (Moses, Paul, and Dr. Luke), but for the most part it was an eclectic group: shepherds, fishermen, a few kings, a high-ranking government employee, and a tax collector. Are these the kinds of people you would choose for the sacred task of Bible writing if you were striving for trustworthiness?

This group would have struggled to collaborate on writing an ad for Craigslist. What are the chances they got everything right when writing history and explaining all things theological? Well, it's better than you might imagine. God didn't let them go rogue and scribble down any wacky thought that passed through their cerebrums. As we will discuss in a minute, the Bible tells us there was a supernatural process through which the Holy Spirit inspired the thoughts of these men as they wrote, in their own vernacular, the books that became our Bible. We know, it sounds a little improbable, maybe even a little wacky. But that's what you get when a supernatural Being writes a book.

How Did God Actually Write the Bible?

To answer the question of whether or not we can trust the Bible, we need to talk about how God wrote the Bible. On one level, this isn't an easy question to answer. God is a spirit, so it's not like he's going to pick up a giant heavenly pen and start writing his book. And forget the image from the classic (and somewhat cheesy) movie *The Ten Commandments*, starring Charlton Heston as a buffed and bearded Moses. Despite Cecil DeMille's effort to portray the drama of Moses receiving the Ten Commandments on Mount Sinai, God didn't carve the words on the stone tablets with his finger.

On another level, it's not all that difficult to understand how God wrote the Bible. He delegated the job to that ragtag group of forty "authors" spread over the span of 1,600 years. These were flawed people, to be sure, but they weren't incompetent. They were intelligent and devoted and fully capable of following God's method for bringing his words to life. In addition, God used other processes to ensure the trustworthiness of his Word. In fact, you could say God used three different but related "links" in a chain that brought his words and his message to us: inspiration, canonization, and transmission.

Link #1: Inspiration

The first link in the chain from God to us is *inspiration*. God did this through the Holy Spirit, the third person of the Trinity. The apostles Paul and Peter explain it this way:

> All Scripture is inspired by God and is useful to teach us what is true and to make us realize what is wrong in our lives. It corrects us when we are wrong and teaches us to do what is right.
>
> 2 Timothy 3:16 NLT

> For prophecy never had its origin in the human will, but prophets, though human, spoke from God as they were carried along by the Holy Spirit.
>
> 2 Peter 1:21

In this context, *inspire* means "to breathe or blow into," and *carried along by* means "moved by." Through the Holy Spirit, God breathed his message into the people who were inspired, moved, and entrusted to record it. Even the dictionary defines *inspiration* as "divine influence."

This wasn't dictation or some kind of automatic writing. The authors of the books in your Bible were inspired by God, but their own personalities and literary gifts were part of the final product. For example, the four Gospels, or biographies of Jesus—told by Matthew, Mark, Luke, and John—tell the same story, but their perspectives are shaped by the personal backgrounds and personalities of each writer. Moreover, it seems that the Holy Spirit inspired each with a different emphasis:

- Matthew focused on Jesus the Messiah, so he put more emphasis on the events and teachings from the life of Jesus, proving that Christ fulfills the predictions in the Old Testament about the Messiah.

- Mark wrote his gospel to the Romans, who had no interest in Old Testament prophecies. They were people of action, so

76

Mark's biography moves along at a rapid pace. Furthermore, he portrayed Jesus as a servant.

• Luke was a doctor, so he emphasized the human side of Christ's nature. Luke was also a Greek, so he wrote with the kind of detail and logic that a Greek reader would have appreciated.

• John's gospel is completely different from the other three. John wanted his readers to understand that Jesus is God, so they could trust him for their salvation.

One more thought about how God inspired human authors to write the Bible. While God didn't dictate the words you read in your Bible, it is reasonable to conclude that the Holy Spirit communicated the words of God—his intent and precise meaning—through the human writers. That's what we mean when we refer to the Bible as God's Word.

QUESTIONS FOR REFLECTION AND DISCUSSION

• What role does inspiration play in the creation of content, such as books, songs, movies, and plays?

• Have you ever been inspired to create an object or accomplish something? What was the result?

• Have you ever felt inspired by God? Do you see this as the working of the Holy Spirit in your life?

Link #2: Canonization

The second link in the chain that brought the Bible from God to us is *canonization*. This is the process by which individual books of the Bible were recognized as being from God. *Canon* is the term used to describe the collection of sixty-six books that eventually made the "cut" to be included in the final version.

The process of canonization is controversial. Some modern scholars believe the church excluded certain books, such as the gospel of Thomas, because they portrayed Jesus as less than divine. The truth is that these books, referred to by traditional scholars as *pseudepigraphical* (or "false ascription"), were excluded because they didn't meet the strict guidelines for canonicity set by a series of church councils that met in the first few centuries after the time of Christ. These guidelines or "checkpoints" were used to determine whether or not a particular book was truly inspired by God:

1. Does it speak with God's authority?
2. Is it written by someone speaking to us as a prophet of God?
3. Does it have the authentic stamp of God?
4. Does it impact us with the power of God?
5. Was it accepted by the people of God?
6. Does it shape or produce communities that reflect the character of God?

This is another stage where you might wonder if the process maintained trustworthiness, or if it broke down as the council members made their determinations. As mentioned, there are skeptics who doubt the reliability of the procedure. You might find it helpful to know that the canon councils did not *declare* a book to be from God. Rather, they *recognized* the divine authority that was already there. Just as the Holy Spirit inspired the Bible authors to write, the Holy Spirit could have directed the decisions of the councils.

Link #3: Transmission

The third link in the chain that brought the Bible from God to us is *transmission*. This describes the total process of transmitting the Scriptures from the early writers—in the original languages and from the original materials they used—to a form later readers could access. Once the total canon of Scripture—the sixty-six books found in your Bible—was recognized as the authoritative

Word of God, the Bible had to be accurately preserved for the future.

This meant the Scriptures had to be laboriously and meticulously copied, translated, recopied, and retranslated so that future generations could not only read the Word of God but also trust it.

QUESTIONS FOR REFLECTION AND DISCUSSION

- Why is it important to know how the Bible came from God to us?
- Compare the process we have just summarized with the way other books of major religions—such as the Book of Mormon and the Qur'an—came to their present forms. What makes the Bible more or less trustworthy than these other books?
- Assuming that all we have said in the preceding section is true and verifiable, what difference does it make to you that the Bible you read was inspired by God?
- What are the implications of the following statement: The Holy Spirit who inspired the original Bible authors is the same Holy Spirit living in those who have a relationship with God through Jesus Christ.

Does the Bible Really Work?

Recently a pastor said, "One of the reasons I personally trust the Bible is because everything it has promised God will do in my life, God has done." This statement is not meant to be a "trump card" superseding all of your questions and doubts about the Bible as the true and authoritative Word of God, but it should spark a question worthy of asking: *Does the Bible work?*

"Does this work?" is a question that must be asked of devices and strategies in virtually every other area of our lives: in relationships, business, parenting, education, government, and even something as mundane as a deodorant you use (maybe especially the deodorant). Truth and reliability can be tested by whether or not something works. Using that same logic, one of the ways we can test the truth and reliability of the Bible is to ask this question. Let's apply it in three different areas of the human experience: the world you inhabit, the faith community you are part of, and the life you live.

Does the Bible work in the world?

In the scope of the universe, galaxy, solar system, and planet we inhabit, the question of whether or not the Bible works may be better stated like this: *Does the Bible reflect reality?* In fact, that is the very definition of truth: *a reflection of the way things really are.*

Detractors would say the Bible doesn't reflect reality. How can a book filled with myths and supernatural accounts be real? It depends on your view of the world. If you hold to the belief that the only reality is *material* reality—that is, only what you can experience with your five senses—then no, the Bible is not completely true because it includes things you can't experience or explain with your five senses. But if you believe there is more to this world than what can be proven scientifically—if there's something *above* nature that best explains how the natural world began and how it works—then the Bible deserves your attention.

This may be difficult for you to think about, but it's important. Pastor Mike Erre points out that the three great "isms"—materialism, naturalism, and consumerism—are what dominate Western life. "They tell us who we are, where we have come from, [and] where we are going,"[1] he writes. The Bible gives an alternate reality. The universe didn't come out of nothing, nor did it create itself. The Bible tells us the world we inhabit was created by God, who is completely outside of the physical reality we experience. As Erre suggests, "If God exists and did create, our view of the world must become much bigger to accommodate the possibility of His work in the world."[2]

- Is "Does the Bible reflect reality?" an appropriate question to test the Bible's trustworthiness about God?
- Do you consider the supernatural to be as real as the natural world? Why or why not?
- Is it possible to believe God is real while simultaneously embracing materialism, naturalism, and consumerism?
- What does all of this have to do with whether or not the Bible works in the world?

Does the Bible work in community?

Now we're going from the macro of the universe to the micro of the community you gather with to grow in your relationships with others, even as you grow together in your relationship with God. If you're not quite there yet—if you are not yet part of a community of faith—that's okay. Hang in there. Your interaction with these concepts and questions may eventually help you determine whether or not you should become a part of one.

Because the Bible is about God (not you, sorry), its primary purpose is to show us God in all his triune glory, including his glorious plan to rescue us in Christ Jesus. (If the word *triune* is a bit puzzling, feel free to jump to chapter 9. Otherwise, here's what it means: God exists in three persons: Father, Son, and Holy Spirit.)

Jesus showed his disciples (the community of believers) how everything written in the Scriptures reveals him. He told them, "You are my witnesses of these things." When you are in community with other believers, and you study the Bible together, you are continuing in the tradition of those who are witnesses of God and his word in their lives—both the written word and the living Word, Jesus Christ.

To a group of believers, that Bible is not an antiquated rule book. The Bible comes alive in the community of believers as if it were "a letter from Christ . . . written not with ink but with the Spirit of the living God, not on tablets of stone but on tablets of human hearts," attesting to the reality of God in the world (2 Corinthians 3:3).

Does the Bible work in you?

We've examined the Bible's relevance from the macro to the micro, and now let's consider the personal: Does it work on a personal and practical level? Again, the Bible is about God, not you, but when Jesus said we would be "witnesses of these things," he wasn't just speaking to those few Christians gathered around him nearly two thousand years ago. He was also speaking to us. That's the beauty and the eternal power of the Bible. The reason you can personally apply something written two thousand years ago is because the Bible is a living book. The writer of Hebrews puts it this way:

> For the word of God is alive and active. Sharper than any double-edged sword, it penetrates even to dividing soul and spirit, joints and marrow; it judges the thoughts and attitudes of the heart.
>
> Hebrews 4:12

Yet the Bible won't impose itself on you. For this reality and power to become vital and active in our lives, we need to experience it. And that comes by reading, studying, memorizing, and meditating on it. In short, if the Bible isn't working in you, you're not working on the Bible. G. K. Chesterton famously said, "Christianity has not been tried and found wanting; it has been found difficult and not tried."[3]

The Bible was never meant to be a divine recipe box, where you flip through the pages until you find just what you're looking for. It is much greater and much grander than that. Theologian Peter Leithart writes,

> All Scripture is practical because God breathed all of it to form people, both individuals and community. . . . God's word expands

82

our imagination to grasp more of what's really there and to envision what might be there in the future. The Bible is useful because it opens our eyes, and because it's highly impractical to walk through life with our eyes closed.[4]

Walking Through Life With Our Eyes Open

There's a wonderful story in the Old Testament (2 Kings 6:1–17) about the prophet Elisha and the king of Aram, who was at war with Israel. Because he was a "man of God," Elisha warned the king of Israel time and time again about the battle plans of his enemy. This enraged the king of Aram, so he sent a strong force of men to capture Elisha. They went with horses and chariots and surrounded the city where Elisha and his servant were staying.

Early in the morning, Elisha's servant went out to survey the landscape. He immediately saw that "an army with horses and chariots had surrounded the city." The servant ran to Elisha in fear and said, "Oh no, my lord! What shall we do?"

In one of the classic lines in all of Scripture, Elisha calmly told his servant that the reality of what he could not see was greater than the reality of what he could see. "Don't be afraid," the prophet answered. "Those who are with us are more than those who are with them."

Elisha then asked God to open his servant's eyes to the unseen reality around him, "so that he may see." The servant's eyes were opened, "and he looked and saw the hills full of horses and chariots of fire all around Elisha."

This is what it means to walk through life with our eyes open, being aware of God's presence and work in the world, working out Scripture in community with others, praying for one another, truly loving each other, bearing each other's burdens, trusting God and his Word together. This is when our spiritual eyes are opened to the miraculous reality around us. This is when peace is found, when miracles happen, and when the Word of God makes vital sense of life and spirituality like nothing else. This is when the

Bible becomes completely true to us, giving us the confidence that we can trust what it says about God and his plans for us.

The Danish philosopher and theologian Søren Kierkegaard said that most of us read the Bible the way a mouse tries to remove the cheese from the trap without getting caught. The Bible's trustworthiness won't become apparent if you approach it in such a tentative and cautious manner. If you are wondering or even skeptical about the Bible's reliability, jump into an investigation of it. Put the Bible to the test.

QUESTIONS FOR REFLECTION

- Has God used the Bible to work in your life? If yes, in what ways has your life been impacted? If no, do you think it is possible for God and Jesus, as described in the Bible, to make changes in your life if you were to study the Bible?
- What might those changes look like? Is there a benefit to studying the Bible if you remain undecided about its reliability?
- If you believe it to be trustworthy, is there a greater motivation to read the Bible? What do you expect will happen in your life as you do so?

5

If the Bible Is So Important, Why Is It So Hard to Understand?

Introduction

Every February, I (Chris) am plagued by this big question: Why is the Bible so difficult to understand? You may wonder, *Why February?* Because every year, as I attempt to read through the entire Bible, I hit a major roadblock in February. Reading at a pace of three chapters a day (about what it takes to get through the Bible in a year), I breeze through Genesis and Exodus in the month of January. Time flies as I am immersed in their gripping accounts of creation and the fall, of Noah's ark full of animals and Abraham's near-sacrifice of his son Isaac. The excitement continues with Moses and the burning bush, ten crazy plagues, and the parting of the Red Sea for the harrowing escape of God's chosen people from slavery in Egypt. Epic stuff! What's not to like about these first two books of the Bible?

Then, like a bottom-of-the-ninth-inning bloop single to ruin a crowd-pleasing no-hitter, Leviticus deflates my enthusiasm with its litany of seemingly inane and incomprehensible laws. Nothing says Happy Valentine's Day like those rules about circumcision. And unfortunately, my frustration doesn't end with the Levitical laws. The question—"Why is the Bible so difficult to understand?"— rears its head again when I take a blind leap into the Prophets. And don't even get me started on Revelation.

Does this sound familiar? Even if you've never tackled the formidable task of reading through the Bible in a year, have you ever come across a book or passage in the Bible that seemed so difficult (or just plain strange) that you made a mental note to never darken its pages again?

▪ ▪ ▪

Truth be told, most Christians struggle to read the Bible at times. In fact, if you were to ask most Bible-believing Christians about their Bible reading habits, you would probably get a bunch of blank stares and embarrassed looks. They *want* to tell you they love reading the Bible, but they can't. If they read the Bible at all, they do it out of a sense of duty rather than delight. Most Christians would agree that the Bible's pages are full of wisdom and insight, but many struggle to understand it and often give up in frustration and confusion.

Who's at Fault? The Bible or Us?

Why is the best-selling book of all time—a book we agree was written by God—so difficult to read and comprehend? Why can't it be more like the Harry Potter series, which is twice as long but easy to follow? If God loves us so much and wants us to understand him and his plan to rescue and redeem all of us, why didn't he make his book as easy to understand as a popular novel? Wouldn't that be better for everybody?

86

So did God goof up when writing his book, or are we the ones to blame? Have we failed to understand God and his way of communicating because he is a bad author, or because we are lazy readers? Is it possible that we don't appreciate that great literature isn't always immediately accessible, so we haven't bothered to give the necessary effort? Dr. Seuss is easy to read, but how can you compare his works to a great novel like *War and Peace.* (Okay, we'll admit, we haven't read Tolstoy's classic book either, but you get our point.)

Admitting Our Struggles

All the big questions we wrestle with in this book are good ones, but this chapter's topic is pivotal. If the Bible really is the key to understanding God and his plans for the world and for us, shouldn't we learn to read and understand it? And if we can get better at reading and understanding the Bible, won't that mean we will be better equipped to discover answers to the toughest questions about God and the Christian faith?

Unfortunately, even if you go to church, you will find few people admitting their struggles, particularly when it comes to understanding the Bible. After all, the Bible is the one book pastors preach and teach from every Sunday (in Bible-teaching churches, anyway), and whether or not they read it, Christians have at least one copy in their homes (sometimes multiple copies). It's readily available online, on your phone, in bookstores and hotel rooms, even in truck stops. So *finding* a Bible is not the problem. *Understanding* the Bible is where there's a disconnect, and we're not always willing to face it.

We think it's helpful to talk about where we are in our walks with God—whether we've been in a relationship with God for years, for just a short while, or never. We need to admit that we're not sure how "good" the Good Book is if we can't understand it.

If this book—God's inspired Word—is as vital to our lives as we say it is, then we need the freedom to engage honestly about our difficulties in reading and understanding it. Hopefully this chapter will allow you to take a deep breath and realize you're not alone. We'll provide some helpful suggestions, guidelines, and much-needed encouragement to keep on reading (and wrestling with) the words and the message in God's life-changing book.

QUESTIONS FOR REFLECTION AND DISCUSSION

- Which book(s) of the Bible do you dread reading?
- Which ones do you steer clear of because they are so difficult to understand? (Go ahead and make a list. Nobody's looking, and we guarantee that your list will look a lot like ours!)
- Which books of the Bible are you most interested in? Why?

What the Bible Is Really All About (and What It's Not)

To wrestle with this chapter's question, we need to acknowledge again a crucial insight from last chapter's tough question: "Can I trust what the Bible says about God?" Can you guess what the most crucial part of that question is? Here's your clue: It's the last two words: *about God*. The reason we need to wrestle with the reliability of Scripture is because it's *about God*. You might even say the Bible is God's autobiography. Henrietta Mears put it this way:

> The Bible is one book, one history, one story—His story. Behind 10,000 events stands God, the builder of history, the maker of the ages. You can go down into the minutest detail everywhere and see that there is one great purpose moving through the ages: the eternal design of the Almighty God to redeem a wrecked and ruined world.[1]

Reflect on that for a moment, because this bit of insight will be very helpful as we begin to wrestle with the questions in this chapter.

Where Do You Fit In?

Have you ever been reading the Bible and found yourself longing for it to resonate with you? Or have you ever noticed how your favorite part of a sermon is when the preacher tells you how to apply the words of Scripture in your personal life? It happens to us all the time. And the reason is simple (WARNING—brutal honesty approaching): We too often think the Bible is about *us*. But (and here's the brutal part) it's not. The inescapable truth is that we all want to be the main character in this powerful story, but the equally important truth is that we're not. God is. So it's no wonder we feel left behind by the Bible, particularly in a culture that grants us permission, and even expects us, to be completely focused on ourselves.

The Bible, thankfully, is all about God. And that is very good news. However, while the Bible may not be *about* us, it certainly is *for* us. In fact, one of the unique things about the Bible is how much it focuses on God's human creation. Every single book of the Bible describes how God has interacted with people. He is not a detached deity. Here's how the apostle Paul explains God's personal involvement in the world he created:

> From one man he made all the nations, that they should inhabit the whole earth; and he marked out their appointed times in history and the boundaries of their lands. God did this so that they would seek him and perhaps reach out for him and find him, though he is not far from any one of us.
>
> Acts 17:26–27

Here's how this helps you:

- **Knowing that the Bible is *about* God and *for* you *helps you understand the Bible*.** Once you wrap your mind around the humbling yet critical reality that the Bible is first and foremost a story about God and his work in the world, you will more easily unlock the mysteries within its pages.
- **Knowing that the Bible is *about* God and *for* you *helps you learn how to read the Bible*.** When you ask the question

89

"What do these passages say about God?" before you ask "What do these passages say to me?" you take the first step toward learning how to read the Bible.

Here's the ironic beauty of these principles. As you learn what the Bible says about God, you end up understanding why he created you, what is wrong with you, what God has done about it, and what he asks of you—*all from a story that is NOT actually about you!*

Over the last few years we've read biographies and memoirs about president Abraham Lincoln, pastor and theologian Dietrich Bonhoeffer, coach Tony Dungy, and writer Stephen King. Each person has impacted each of us personally and changed our lives in a significant way. The book about Lincoln shaped thoughts on leadership. Bonhoeffer's was a lesson in courage. Tony Dungy's book was the most personal one in the bunch, and out of the tragedy of his son's death emerged a profound vision for fatherhood. And Stephen King, perhaps the one you would least expect to be inspirational, actually taught all of us valuable tips on how to write so that people are moved and not just informed.

Each of these books is a specific, personal, and true story about someone else, yet they produced benefits for us. The same is true with the Bible (only exponentially and supernaturally so!). The Bible is about someone who far surpasses the likes of presidents, pastors, coaches, and writers, and it can shape us infinitely more than human biographies and memoirs. The Bible is not about us, but it is definitely for us.

QUESTIONS FOR REFLECTION AND DISCUSSION

- How do you feel about the idea that the Bible is about God, not you?
- If you take this to heart, how might it affect the way you read the Bible?
- In your opinion, what are some of the benefits of the Bible's being first and foremost about God? Any drawbacks?

The True Story of God

Before we introduce some simple ways to better read and under-stand the Bible, can we offer you a bit of encouragement? (You might as well say yes, because we're going to anyway!) Reading and understanding the Bible takes time and effort. But like anything beneficial, it's worth the energy. And besides, it's not like you're jumping into the *Hunger Games* trilogy or a cooking blog (as fun and entertaining as they may be). With Scripture you are reading and re-reading the *inspired Word of God*. While the Bible can be entertaining, enthralling, and exciting, the most important thing we can say about the Bible is that it is the true story of who God is, who we are, and why this life matters.

There's a reason why we (and many other Christians these days) speak and write about God's story. It's because all life is captured in story. Stories give voice to who we are, how we act, what we dream about and hope for. If we were to ask you to talk about yourself, how would you respond? With a story, right? If you were to describe the most significant moments in your life, you would tell stories.

As it turns out, we are storytellers because God is a storyteller. So to more easily understand Scripture, we need to take it as it is: a remarkable epic story about God and the universe in which we live. The best part is that we are already familiar with this glorious tale. In fact, many of the stories we love follow God's grand plot line. It's why they resonate with us.

God's story includes the classic elements of creation, fall, and redemption that inform the plots of such well-known stories as the *Odyssey* by Homer, *The Wizard of Oz* by L. Frank Baum, and *The Lord of the Rings* by J. R. R. Tolkien. In each of these stories, there is a hero who is called to an adventure, faces a road of trials and death, and is then resurrected or reborn, thereby transforming the world.

The great Christian writer and literary scholar C. S. Lewis gave the reason these stories (or myths, as he called them) about heroes

91

are common across time and cultures: God put them there. Literally, God has spoken to us through the common myths to make us familiar with, and to point to, the one true story, or "true myth." According to Lewis, the Myth that became Fact—the incarnation (God coming in the flesh as Jesus), tests, relationships, trials, death, and resurrection of Jesus—is the one story that has the power to give us life.[2] And it is that big story we must begin with if the Bible is to be less difficult to read and if we ever hope to understand and enjoy the smaller chapters and scenes within it.

> ### QUESTIONS FOR REFLECTION AND DISCUSSION
> - Pick one of your favorite characters from a movie or a book—it could be Frodo, Luke Skywalker, Dorothy—and identify the elements that parallel the life of Jesus. We're not trying to be disrespectful. Far from it! We just want you to see how stories familiar to all of us parallel the one true story of Jesus.

Go Big

The expression "Go big or go home" may not be the first phrase you think of when you think about the Bible, but it applies nicely. Many people—okay, *most* people—read the Bible like a dictionary or a recipe box. They don't think about reading it from beginning to end. Instead, they go to certain verses, phrases, words, or formulas to get their spiritual pick-me-up. But while "*all* Scripture is God-breathed and is useful for teaching, rebuking, correcting and training in righteousness" (2 Timothy 3:16, emphasis added), we can short-circuit God's intended message if we ignore the Bible's big picture.

If you want full impact, you have to start with the full story. Without it, the verses are more like snapshots: They may inspire you with their beauty, but you will miss their deepest and truest meaning. So our first step in understanding the Bible (and in turn the God of the Bible) is to start with God's big story.

What is that big story? We're glad you asked. There are six major acts:

- *Act 1: Creation*—God, out of his great love and infinite creativity, spoke all of creation into being. And it was flawless. Absolutely flawless.
- *Act 2: The Fall*—God's most-loved part of creation—you and us—took the role of being God into our own hands. We rebelled against his good design and instruction. That rebellion broke our relationship with God, with each other, and with his creation beyond our ability to repair it.
- *Act 3: Israel*—God, unwilling to watch us die in our rebellion, chose an ordinary people to display for the world his extraordinary love, forgiveness, and way of life. And it was through the Jewish people that he sent a Savior.
- *Act 4: Jesus*—In the final act of redemption, God came in the flesh as Jesus of Nazareth. He rescued and redeemed us by his life and death, and he proved he is Lord of all by his resurrection.
- *Act 5: The Church*—Since then, God, by his Spirit, has empowered his followers to introduce everyone to Jesus Christ and join in his mission to heal this broken world.
- *Act 6: New Creation*—In the end (or maybe just the beginning!), Jesus will return to rescue his bride, the church, once and for all. And there will be no more sadness, crying, pain, or death. And God will be with us forever (hallelujah and amen!).

If you are familiar with the Bible or Christianity, these six "Acts" will likely ring a bell. If you are not, this is the place to start. Can you see the story arc? Can you see in it how God—who created something good, allowed us the freedom to mess it up, but loves us too much to leave us alone in the havoc we wreaked—is writing a big story for his glory and our good? This is our first key to understanding the Bible: Start big.

QUESTIONS FOR REFLECTION AND DISCUSSION

- How would you briefly outline the story of your life?
- How would this particular moment in time—your family and friends, beliefs and questions, joys and sorrows, successes and failures—fit into that outline?
- Is the story of the Bible what you thought it would be? Why or why not?
- How does it feel to know that you are living in God's big story?

Now Go Medium

Would you agree that starting with the big picture is helpful, but still leaves room for some questions and doesn't fully solve the difficulty of reading the Bible? Yeah, us too. So here are a few more questions worth wrestling with in our effort to better understand the Bible. These questions deal with *context* and *genre*.

Context

What if each book in the Bible was written to specific people for a specific time for a specific reason? And what if we could learn to understand each of those? The answer to both of these questions is rhetorical, because each book was written for a specific audience for a specific reason, and it's important that we take these contextual issues into account when we read the Bible.

The most basic type of context to look for in any book of the Bible is *historical*. Specifically, what is the *occasion* and *purpose* of each book? It's important to know what was going on at the time, both with the people to whom the book was written, as well as with the surrounding culture. Most of the time you will find the answers to this question in the book itself. At other times you will need the help of outside resources. We provide some help on this later.

There's another type of context, commonly referred to as *literary*. The principle is that words have meaning only in sentences, and any sentence only has meaning in the context of the sentences that come before and after.

Context at the movies: A couple of years ago, Chris and his wife, Kerry, went to the movies to see *Catching Fire*, the second installment of the Hunger Games series. As they settled into their seats for the "pre-show entertainment" (that's a fancy name for commercials), they noticed that the entire theater was full of moms and dads and their young kids. Very young kids. Most of them were under the age of seven. As any of us would have done, they began to judge those parents harshly. Chris leaned toward his wife to whisper, "Can you believe they are going to let their five-year-old daughter watch a movie about an annual competition where people kill other people for sport?"

As they sat on their moral high horses, their self-righteousness was interrupted by the previews (all of which were for animated features), and their confusion deepened as the screen lit up with a six-minute mini-movie starring Mickey Mouse and Goofy. Finally, it clicked. Chris put down his popcorn, walked out the theater door, looked up at the marquee for the movie, and saw it clear as day: "Theater #4: FROZEN." The parents around them had not used poor judgment by bringing their kids to the wrong movie. It was they who were lost and sitting in the wrong theater! Chris and Kerry ate some humble pie and quickly walked to the correct theater, where they had a good laugh and enjoyed the feature they had intended to see.

This silly illustration paints a good picture about the power of context. In the context of the movie *Catching Fire*, small children and animated previews made no sense. But in the context of the movie *Frozen*, kids and cartoons were a perfect fit. The message—the previews, the pre-show entertainment—made sense for the right audience. Once Chris and Kerry understood the intended audience, all confusion was gone.

The same is true for the Bible. When we understand Paul's context—he wrote his letters in a much different time (the first century), to six different churches, each facing different circumstances—we can begin to grasp the intended meaning, both for the original audience and for us today. The same goes for Genesis and Malachi, Matthew and Revelation, and every book in between.

Admittedly, this is going to take some work. Thankfully, there is outside help available at your fingertips (literally). There are online tools as well as old-school tools, such as Bible dictionaries, Bible handbooks, and Bible commentaries. For starters, we suggest that you invest in a study Bible, which will provide context and background material for every book of the Bible.

Genre

What if God's epic story was broken up into sixty-six separate books, many of which were written in different literary styles? How important would it be for us to learn to understand those different genres? Again, these are rhetorical questions, because the answer is, *Very important!*

The word *genre* simply means "literary form." You don't read a history book and a book of poetry in the same way, just as the writers don't write them in the same way. History is literal, while poetry is figurative, so you treat them differently. The same goes for the books of the Bible, which contain at least five genres or literary forms:

1. *Narrative:* Emphasizes stories to illustrate truth. The first chunk of the Old Testament (Genesis to Ezra) is narrative. Also, the four Gospels and the book of Acts are narrative.

2. *Poetic:* Conveys truth through our imaginations and emotions. There's a reason why the book of Psalms is among the most popular books in the Bible. We identify deeply with the emotions expressed by the writers.

3. *Proverbial:* These pithy sayings give moral truth and advice, often in the form of a story. The entire book of Proverbs follows this literary form (duh), but you can find examples through metaphors, similes, and parables in other parts of Scripture.

4. **Prophetic:** Much of the Bible contains prophecy, but not the kind you think. Most of the prophets in the Old Testament conveyed God's truth to the people and their leaders (called "forthtelling"). From time to time the prophets predicted events that would occur in the future (called "foretelling"). The book of Revelation actually fits into a subcategory of prophecy called "apocalyptic." This kind of literature talks about the cataclysmic events that will occur at the end of the world.

5. **Didactic:** Teaches truth in a direct manner. The letters of Paul are a prime example.

QUESTIONS FOR REFLECTION

- What are some other scenarios in life where context matters?
- Have you ever had an experience similar to Chris and Kerry's in the movie theater? What happened?
- What will you gain by exploring the context and genre of a particular book of the Bible? Does this approach seem exciting, daunting, helpful, or something else altogether? Why?

Finally, Go Small

We love going small. One of Bruce and Stan's best-selling books—in fact it's a whole series of books—has the word *small* in it. *God Is in the Small Stuff* was the first, and they have written more than a few devotionals and other books filled with bite-sized truth and applications from God's Word so that anybody can understand them. Chris has done the same thing in two devotional books he has written: *Easter Is Coming* and *Christmas Is Coming.*

So it shouldn't surprise you that the three of us believe writing in small chunks and quoting single Bible verses is more appealing to today's reader than writing long books and quoting long portions of Scripture. We live in a world of 140-character tweets, Facebook updates, and Instagram. Everyone seems to be busier these days, and one of the activities people make less time for is reading.

As a result, people are looking for content that is easily accessible on their mobile devices so they can read wherever and whenever they want. And they want their nonfiction content in easy-to-digest portions. We get that. But we also realize that there is a disadvantage to reading small if that's all you do. Especially when it comes to God's Word.

Earlier in this chapter, we talked about literary context and how important it is to read a verse in the context of the passage, chapter, and book where it's found. Admittedly, a verse like this one from Jeremiah, one of the most quoted verses in the Bible, brings great comfort to people and reflects the mercy and goodness of God:

> "For I know the plans I have for you," declares the Lord, "plans to prosper you and not harm you, plans to give you hope and a future."
>
> Jeremiah 29:11

There's just one problem. That verse by the prophet Jeremiah is part of a letter written to the Jewish exiles who were in captivity in Babylon 2,500 years ago. God's "plans" were for their welfare and return to their homeland, but only after 70 years in exile. That's a very different meaning from the one modern readers often assign to that verse.

We don't mean to dampen your enthusiasm for the good plans and promises of God scattered throughout the Bible. We aren't suggesting that you read the Bible only as a history book with no application and meaning for you. We'll say it again. God's Word is living and active, and the same Holy Spirit who inspired Jeremiah to write his prophetic book lives in those who have put their faith in God through Jesus Christ. But you will understand more about the great God who created you and loves you and saved you and has plans for you—if you take the time and make the effort to read the Bible diligently, paying attention to the details. That's what we mean by going small.

As we've already said, understanding the Bible by learning to read it takes time and effort. But that's what serious disciples of Jesus Christ do. They are *learners* (that's the literal meaning of *disciple*) who follow Jesus with a deep desire to know God and develop into the people he wants us to become. It's not a walk in the park, but if you keep at it, your time and effort will bear fruit worth tasting. Here is Paul's advice to his protégé, the young pastor Timothy:

> Do your best to present yourself to God as one approved, a worker who does not need to be ashamed and who correctly handles the word of truth.
>
> 2 Timothy 2:15

QUESTIONS FOR REFLECTION

- Choose an impactful moment, relationship, or experience in your life, and try to capture all of its meaning in twenty words or less. Can you do it? What are the drawbacks?
- What do you think are the pros and cons of reading and digesting just a few Bible verses at a time?

Practical Tips for Reading and Understanding the Bible

There are several excellent books we recommend to help you read and study the Bible. But for now, we want to give you some practical ideas and tools so you will better understand the Bible and find God in its pages.

- *Read it all.* Read a book of the Bible in its entirety—in one sitting, or over several days or weeks if the book is longer—so you can fully grasp the author's intent from beginning to end.
- *Read it slowly and prayerfully.* Don't read for information, but for formation.

- *Read it out loud.* Like you're reading a play, not a textbook.
- *Read it with others.* Two heads are better than one. More people ask better questions.
- *Read a study Bible or commentary.* These tools will help you understand a book, especially with regard to context and genre.
- *Read it chronologically.* The Bible follows a chronological order—sort of. Sometimes the story line jumps out of order, but there is a historical flow that will help you understand the "whole counsel of God" (Acts 20:27 ESV).

The Book of Life

As we mentioned above, the Bible is the best-selling, most distributed book of all time, and it shows no signs of slowing down. According to *The Economist*, "100 [million] copies are sold or given away every year" and "Gideon's International gives away a Bible every second,"[3] so there is something very special about it. Obviously. You wouldn't be reading this book written by us unless you really wanted to tackle the difficulties of reading the book written by God.

We agree with the apostle John, one of Jesus' best friends, who wrote that God's Word was "written that you may believe that Jesus is the Messiah, the Son of God, and that by believing you may have life in his name" (John 20:31). That's why this question—"Why is the Bible so difficult to understand?"—is such an important one to wrestle with. We don't have new life because millions of Bibles were printed this year, or because we own one, or because we carry ours to church. Lives are changed because we *read* the Bible and seek with all our God-given mind and resources to understand it. And it can be done!

But as the saying goes, Rome wasn't built in a day. So we start big by understanding God's grand narrative in the Bible. Then we go medium by learning to grasp the context and genre of each book we read. Finally, we go small, gaining life and wisdom from individual verses and passages as we understand them within their greater context. February—or Leviticus—no longer has to be the point in our year when our Bible reading grinds to a halt. With some effort, the right resources, and a Bible-believing community, understanding the Bible is not only possible but is a rewarding and life-changing pursuit.

QUESTIONS FOR REFLECTION

- Of the six practical tips offered in this chapter, which one or two are most appealing to you?
- For most of us, why is it necessary to develop some kind of discipline or technique when it comes to reading the Bible?
- What are some benefits to developing a lifelong habit of Bible reading and study?

6

Why Does God Seem So Violent While Jesus Is So Loving?

Introduction

Kara would be a terrible poker player. Her expressions reveal exactly what she's thinking at the exact moment she thinks it, so you can read her like a book. One Wednesday morning we met on the church patio for coffee, and as I (Chris) approached the table, I could tell she was already engaged in a mental tug-of-war. She stared at the table with furrowed brow, and her lips pursed like she had just downed a piece of sour candy. As her young adult pastor, I couldn't wait to hear what was on her mind. It didn't take long to find out.

"Morning, Kara!" I said as I approached the table. "Whatcha thinking about?" Skipping the typical morning greeting, she replied, "So I've been thinking about the survey you sent out." And just like that, we were off and running.

The survey she referred to was an open-ended questionnaire I emailed to the young adults at our church, asking them to anonymously share any questions they had about a dozen or so subjects related to God, the Bible, faith, and life. (Their responses became the kindling for this book series.) I wanted to know the kinds of topics they were wrestling with, and they provided honest responses. One question in particular was rattling Kara's cage.

"There's a question that's bothered me for a long time," she continued. "How can God of the Old Testament be the same as God in the New Testament? He seems so angry and vindictive and violent in the Old Testament. And in the New Testament, he's so, well, nice! He's kind. I mean, he's Jesus!" Kara's question was familiar. In one way or another, several other survey responders had asked the same thing. She finished with, "What changes? How does he go from wiping out entire cities and races to saving the world through the love and sacrifice of his Son? It feels like two different Gods, and I'm not sure I can be in a relationship with the first one."

Kara let out a heavy sigh and took her first breath since beginning her question. I did the same. When both of us breathed again, I looked her in the eyes, smiled, and said, "Those are very good questions, Kara. Very good questions indeed."

▪ ▓ ▪

Kara's questions—like other questions in this book—are valid because they are honest and legitimate on multiple levels. For those already inclined to reject Christianity and who are looking for reasons to support their predisposition, the apparent contradiction between the vengeance of the Old Testament and the love of the New Testament only serves to reinforce their view.

Those who are sincerely searching to find God (or trying to determine if God exists at all) might have doubts about being in a relationship with someone they perceive to be jealous, unjust, and unforgiving. If those qualities are true, why pursue him at all?

Then there are the rest of us, wholehearted followers of Jesus who are onboard with bringing Christ's compassion and peace into the world. But we sometimes wonder if the seemingly archaic and irrelevant commands of the Old Testament have any relevance to our lives today. In fact, can't we just skip over those parts that seem to portray God in a negative light?

A Quick Bible Overview

Before we dig deep into the topic of this chapter, let's handle one procedural matter and discuss a few Bible basics. First, as to the procedure we'll follow in this chapter: We'll save a lot of space if we abbreviate "Old Testament" with a simple "OT." We also might use the abbreviation "NT," but you'll have to guess what that stands for.

Next, let's make sure we have a common understanding of the basics of the Bible's composition:

1. The OT and the NT are not separate books. They are each a compendium of many separate books, of which thirty-nine are compiled in the OT, and twenty-seven are in the NT. Together, these sixty-six books compose a single volume known as the Bible (which means "book"). The sixty-six books of the Bible were written over a period of approximately 1,600 years by forty different authors.

2. "Old" and "New" are not the best adjectives, because the OT and the NT are both old. The thirty-nine books of the OT were written during the approximate period of 2000 BC to 400 BC. The twenty-seven books of the NT were written during the approximate period of AD 45 to AD 95. So even the "New" Testament is more than nineteen centuries old.

3. The OT and the NT each focus primarily on different time frames. At the risk of oversimplifying, we'll just say that the OT covers the time from the creation of the world and humanity but stops a few hundred years before the birth of Jesus. The NT begins with the birth of Christ, covers events of his life—including his death, burial, resurrection, and

105

return to heaven—and then records the early history and teachings of the Christian church.

From these "basics," it is easy to see how Kara's questions arise. For example, there are thousands of years between many of the events reported in the OT and the beginning of the NT. Is it possible that God's attitude changed in the intervening years? Perhaps he started out in the OT as cantankerous and irascible; but then, maybe, he mellowed out over a couple thousand years, so in NT times he sent Jesus down to earth for some public relations damage control.

Or could it be that over the thousands of years as God's plan for humanity unfolded, God dealt with humans in contrasting ways, much as a parent might alter disciplinary techniques as a child moves through different stages of development? And let's not overlook the multiple authors who contributed to the Bible. Like reporters at any newsworthy event, each author may have had a particular focus or angle for his own report. Do all differences in reporting automatically qualify as contradictions, or should differences be evaluated within the context of the respective messages the authors were seeking to convey?

To wrestle with Kara's questions, let's begin by examining the nature and character of God in the context of this question: Is OT God the opposite of NT Jesus?

QUESTIONS FOR REFLECTION AND DISCUSSION

- If someone asked you to describe the "God of the Old Testament," how would you respond?
- In what ways do you consider "Jesus of the New Testament" to be different?
- Do you think that you know one of them better than the other, and if so, why is that?
- As you read the Bible, do ideas get "lost in translation," or can you pretty much follow what's going on?

- Describe, in one or a few sentences, the overall message of the Bible.
- Do you have a favorite book of the Bible?

God the Father and Jesus the Son . . . One and the Same God

The characterization that God in the Old Testament is angry and violent but that Jesus in the New Testament is loving and peaceful fits well with our polarized times. The drastic contrast in this apparent conflict between the Testaments is easily added to the list of other battles in our society. As a culture, we are accustomed to contrasting differences between opposite points of view: liberals vs. conservatives, the religious vs. the humanists, vegans vs. carnivores, and iPhones vs. Androids. Like the other categories on the list, the OT God vs. the NT Jesus disparities are exaggerated by oversimplification, generalization, and a lack of information.

People who have little or no familiarity with the Bible can easily join the debate because the issue has been cast in terms of polar opposites. In the OT God is violent, but in the NT Jesus is tender and kind; in the OT God is wrathful, but in the NT he is forgiving; the OT presents a God of war, but in the NT he's all about peace; God is mean and Jesus is nice; God is racist, sexist, and patriarchal, but Jesus is tender, kind, and all-inclusive. As a society, we've managed to envision God against Jesus in the most crucial heavyweight grudge bout of all time, and you can almost hear the announcer now. . . .

In this corner—weighing A LOT—is the Creator of the universe, the destroyer of sinners, a jealous, hateful, vicious killer—it's GOD! And in the opposite corner, of average human weight and size, is his opponent—the Redeemer of mankind, the forgiver of all, the sweet pacifist, lover of children, women, and the poor—it's JESUS!

107

All that's left for us to do is to select which combatant we are going to cheer for.

But the entire notion of OT God being opposite of NT Jesus violates the clear teaching of Scripture. One of the most important truths in the Bible involves a word that isn't even in the Bible: *Trinity*. Essentially, the Trinity describes the three distinct persons who make up the God of the Bible: God the Father, Jesus Christ the Son, and the Holy Spirit. The concept of the Trinity has plenty of questions surrounding it, so we'll postpone an in-depth discussion until chapter 9. But the point relevant to Kara's questions is this: God the Father and Jesus the Son are one and the same, and in all respects they are identical. They don't have different personalities. There is absolutely no difference between their sensitivities, attitudes, and character . . . not because they are so much alike, but because they are the same God.

During his three-year public ministry, NT Jesus never tried to separate or distinguish himself from OT God. In fact, it was just the opposite. Repeatedly, Jesus emphasized that he and "the Father" were one and the same. Look at these instances from John 10:

- In a debate with the Jewish leaders, Jesus referred to himself as the Good Shepherd (v. 11), which would have reminded everyone of the revered Psalm 23 written by King David, which begins, "The Lord [OT God] is my shepherd. . . ."
- In another encounter, Jesus was asked flat out if he was the Messiah. He began his answer by saying, "I did tell you, but you do not believe. The works I do in my Father's name testify about me, but you do not believe because you are not my sheep. My sheep listen to my voice; I know them, and they follow me. I give them eternal life" (vv. 25–28). And just to make sure there was no ambiguity about his answer, he finishes with "I and the Father are one" (v. 30).
- The people around Jesus completely understood that Jesus was claiming equality with God by making his "the Father

and I are one" statement. The very next verse states that his Jewish opponents in the crowd picked up rocks to stone him. Jesus was able to escape, but before he did his attackers made it clear they wanted to kill him "for blasphemy, because you, a mere man, claim to be God" (v. 35).

Think of the implications of this. What happens to the construct of Kara's questions if OT God and NT Jesus are one and the same? That would mean that we can't attribute certain characteristics to OT God while assigning different (and usually opposite) characteristics to NT Jesus. If OT God is righteous and forceful when dealing with sin, then we must expect that NT Jesus is the same. And if NT Jesus is loving and caring, so is OT God.

QUESTIONS FOR REFLECTION AND DISCUSSION

- In John 14:8-9, you will find this conversation:

  Philip said, "Lord, show us the Father and that will be enough for us." Jesus answered: "Don't you know me, Philip, even after I have been among you such a long time? Anyone who has seen me has seen the Father."

  What do you think Jesus meant by the "Anyone who has seen me has seen the Father" comment?
- What do you think the disciples thought he was saying?
- What do you know about Jesus that could inform your opinion about his Father?

Maybe our greatest error has been to think of OT God and NT Jesus as two and separate beings. Instead, we should be speaking of the "God of the Bible" (ahh, new terminology: Bible God). This tweaks Kara's question a bit. It is no longer about seeking an explanation of personality differences between OT God and NT Jesus. Rather, the inquiry becomes more refined. If Kara was reading along with you, she might put it this way:

Okay, I get the one-and-the-same God thing. But that still doesn't change my impression that this "Bible God" is always very angry in the Old Testament, but always loving and gentle in the New Testament. And if God changes, I'm a little worried about that, because I'm not sure I want to hitch my spiritual wagon to a God who has such wide mood swings.

Ah, Kara, you've done it again. More good questions indeed.

Does God Change?

The principle that God the Father and Jesus the Son are the same God has led us to wonder if God can change. After all, between portions of the Old Testament and the writings of the New Testament, he would have had thousands of years to do so. Even our own maturity from adolescence to adulthood doesn't take that long to develop. Is it reasonable to expect that God can change over several millennia? Maybe he got tired and frustrated in dealing with sinful humanity in the Old Testament, so he simply decided to change his approach in the New Testament.

The Bible is clear on the issues of God's changeability. It doesn't happen. Theologians use the term *immutability* to describe God's steadfast, never-changing nature. In a layperson's terms, God is the same yesterday, today, and tomorrow. Here are just two of the many verses that confirm this aspect of God's character:

> I the Lord do not change.
>
> Malachi 3:6

> Every good and perfect gift is from above, coming down from the Father of the heavenly lights, who does not change like shifting shadows.
>
> James 1:17

The doctrine of God's immutability won't resolve Kara's question about the contrasting depiction of God in the Old and New Testaments, but it should be a big relief to know that we are dealing

110

with a God who won't change the rules on us. The Bible reveals him as a God who abhors evil and sinfulness, and he will always be so. The Bible also presents God as forgiving, merciful, and gracious. We should take great comfort in knowing those characteristics are everlasting (and not just limited to the days when he happens to be "in a good mood").

QUESTIONS FOR REFLECTION

- Would it bother you if God could change?
- What would you be worried about?
- What comfort do you find in knowing that he doesn't change?

Just When You Weren't Expecting It
(That's why it's called a pop quiz)

It's time to begin unpacking Kara's revised question (the one we think she would be asking if she had been reading this chapter): "Why *is* this 'Bible God' always very angry in the Old Testament, but always loving and gentle in the New Testament?" Let's start with a pop quiz.

Below are six passages from the Bible, without citation to their book/chapter/verse. Some are from the Old Testament, and some are from the New Testament. Without peeking at the answers in the text farther below, guess whether each passage comes from the Old Testament or from the New Testament. Ready . . . begin.

1. He has shown you, O mortal, what is good. And what does the Lord require of you? To act justly and to love mercy and to walk humbly with your God.

2. "Then he will say to those on his left, 'Depart from me, you who are cursed, into the eternal fire prepared for the devil

and his angels. For I was hungry and you gave me nothing to eat, I was thirsty and you gave me nothing to drink, I was a stranger and you did not invite me in, I needed clothes and you did not clothe me, I was sick and in prison and you did not look after me.' . . . Then they will go away to eternal punishment, but the righteous to eternal life."

3. "But if a wicked person turns away from all the sins they have committed and keeps all my decrees and does what is just and right, that person will surely live; they will not die. None of the offenses they have committed will be remembered against them. Because of the righteous things they have done, they will live. Do I take any pleasure in the death of the wicked? declares the Sovereign Lord. Rather, am I not pleased when they turn from their ways and live?"

4. Seek good, not evil, that you may live. Then the Lord God Almighty will be with you, just as you say he is. Hate evil, love good; maintain justice in the courts.

5. And I saw an angel standing in the sun, who cried in a loud voice to all the birds flying in midair, "Come, gather together for the great supper of God, so that you may eat the flesh of kings, generals, and the mighty, of horses and their riders, and the flesh of all people, free and slave, great and small." Then I saw the beast and the kings of the earth and their armies gathered together to wage war against the rider on the horse and his army. But the beast was captured, and with it the false prophet who had performed the signs on its behalf. With these signs he had deluded those who had received the mark of the beast and worshiped its image. The two of them were thrown alive into the fiery lake of burning sulfur. The rest were killed with the sword coming out of the mouth of the rider on the horse, and all the birds gorged themselves on their flesh.

6. When God saw what they did and how they turned from their evil ways, he relented and did not bring on them the destruction he had threatened.

As you were so perceptive to quickly notice, the passages in the pop quiz either described God's kind and gracious nature or focused on his more stern attributes.

If you adhered to Kara's generalization that all angry God stuff came from the Old Testament and all nice God stuff was from the New Testament, then you gave an incorrect answer for every passage. Here are the Bible references for each of the passages above in the order they were given:

1. Micah 6:8 (OT)—nice God
2. Matthew 25:41–43, 46 (NT)—angry God
3. Ezekiel 18:21–23 (OT)—nice God
4. Amos 5:14–15 (OT)—nice God
5. Revelation 19:17–21 (NT)—angry God
6. Jonah 3:10 (OT)—nice God

QUESTIONS FOR REFLECTION AND DISCUSSION

- After reading these passages, did you learn something about God that you didn't already know?
- We have a tendency to focus on verses and passages from Scripture that talk about the God we want, which isn't a bad thing. But what happens when we avoid those passages that show God for who he really is?
- Why is it important to get the "whole picture" of God?

The Whole Picture

You probably anticipated our ploy and scored well using counterintuitive answers. But let's not miss the lesson of this pop quiz.

The Old and New Testaments do not present one-sided, opposite depictions of the Bible's God. To the contrary, the Old Testament shows the *full* panoply of God's character, and the New Testament also shows the *complete* spectrum of God's attributes. In *both* Testaments, God the Father and Jesus the Son are described as compassionate, peace-loving, forgiving, patient, kind, and judging. And they are also portrayed as being wrathful, powerful, and violent against sin and evil. God's approach to those he loves and his approach to sin and evil do not change from the OT to the NT. So it is not surprising that:

- *In the Old Testament*, God the Father is often portrayed as a shepherd who lovingly and sacrificially cares for his sheep. This analogy is used in Psalm 23, in which you'll find no harsh treatment, but only providence and tenderness extended to the sheep (which, in the extension of the analogy, are people who follow God as their shepherd). As you read this Psalm, can't you just imagine that you would enjoy life as a sheep of this Shepherd:

  > God, my shepherd! I don't need a thing.
  > You have bedded me down in lush meadows,
  >   you find me quiet pools to drink from.
  > True to your word,
  >   you let me catch my breath
  >   and send me in the right direction.
  > Even when the way goes through Death Valley,
  > I'm not afraid
  >   when you walk at my side.
  > Your trusty shepherd's crook
  >   makes me feel secure.
  > You serve me a six-course dinner
  >   right in front of my enemies.
  > You revive my drooping head;
  >   my cup brims with blessing.
  > Your beauty and love chase after me
  >   every day of my life.

> I'm back home in the house of God
>> for the rest of my life.
>>> Psalm 23 THE MESSAGE

All of a sudden, OT God seems much more compassionate and tenderhearted than Kara ever imagined.

• *In the New Testament*, Christ's vehemence against sin and evil is blatantly revealed. In Matthew 21, it is reported that Jesus visited the temple and was enraged that this place intended for worship was being used for illegal and fraudulent transactions, all of which were allowed under the auspices of the Jewish religious leaders. Worshipers were required to purchase an animal for sacrifice, but they could offer only "temple approved" animals, which they were forced to purchase with "temple currency." So, for example, the moneychangers jacked up the exchange rate, and the pigeon merchants overcharged for defective, scrawny birds (which technically didn't meet the rigorous standards for a sacrificial offering). The fact that many of these worshipers were poor had no impact on the mercenary merchants and Jewish leaders who shared in the scams. As Jesus surveyed this travesty of justice, this sacrilege in the temple, and the abuse of the poor and innocent, he could not contain his righteous anger:

> Jesus went straight to the Temple and threw out everyone who had set up shop, buying and selling. He kicked over the tables of loan sharks and the stalls of dove merchants. He quoted this text: My house was designated a house of prayer; you have made it a hangout for thieves.
>> Matthew 21:12–13 THE MESSAGE

Imagine that. Jesus, the meek and mild, has a Hulk-like moment. In the defense of the poor and in honor of God's holiness, Jesus single-handedly demolishes the kiosks of the

115

merchants and moneychangers. Then he physically drives all of them out of the temple courtyard. His outrage and ferocity were so intimidating (and effective) that not a single person dared to oppose him, either then or later.

Jesus displayed more fury and forcefulness than Kara ever expected to find in the New Testament.

QUESTIONS FOR REFLECTION AND DISCUSSION

- Can you think of an instance from the Old Testament that shows the kindness of God? (If you can't think of anything else, here's a hint: "Let my people go.")
- Next, from the New Testament, can you think of an instance when Christ comes across as stern and confrontational? (Hint: How did Jesus feel about the Pharisees?)

Let's regroup and take stock of where we are in this discussion before moving on:

- There's no difference between OT God and NT Jesus. There is only the one and the same God throughout the Bible.
- God doesn't change overnight or over time. So we see God's love for his people and his hatred of sin in both the OT and the NT.

To Kara's credit, her questions arose from what is blatantly obvious to anyone who has a passing familiarity with the Bible. The OT and the NT seem very different. The disparity is striking, and almost alarming, to someone (such as Kara) who is honestly trying to make sense of the incongruity between the two Testaments. Any dissimilarity between them, however, can't be attributable to differences in God (who is immutable). So why or how is it that so many of us read the Bible and get confused when trying to reconcile the OT with the NT?

The answer may be in the Bible itself. After all, this is God we are dealing with—a God who can be known but never fully comprehended. Maybe it shouldn't be surprising that we need to know more about God in order to fully appreciate his Word (the Bible). An in-depth study of any one of God's attributes would be helpful, but in the next section we'll just focus on the one that Kara zeroed in on: love (you remember, the love that she felt was prevalent in the NT but absent in the OT).

Our View of God's Love May Be Too Restricted

Imagine a "person on the street" interview in which a guy at random is asked, "What do you love?" His answer could possibly be, "Uh, I love breakfast burritos, I love my wife, and I love my Green Bay Packers." While the same word is used for each, hopefully the degree and depth of his love is drastically different, at least with respect to his wife. But we live in a culture where the concept of *love* does not have a universally accepted meaning, and it has become a generic, overused term that further dilutes and obscures its meaning. Perhaps the reason many of us struggle with the full picture of God (in both Testaments) is because our definition of love is too small.

Many people conceptualize God as a doddering grandfather, permissive yet still protective, but by no means a disciplinarian. He's a "Do whatever makes you happy, just so long as nobody gets hurt!" kind of grandfather God. If that is our perception of God, then it distorts our impression of what we expect of God's love. In that view, God should allow us to do anything that is "true to ourselves" just as long as nobody gets hurt. If we bring these expectations to our reading of the Bible, then we will be quick to embrace the NT statements that "God is love." And conversely, we will be resistant to OT verses that speak of obedience (including the "thou shalt . . ." and the "thou shalt not . . ." verses that offend our desire for freedom of self-expression).

Because we want God's love to be permissive, we are attracted to verses in the NT that emphasize God's forgiveness and God's "gift of eternal life" (Romans 6:23). But that same notion of God's love being permissive causes us to gloss over the NT references that "the wages of sin is death" (also Romans 6:23).

On the flip side, if we constrict God's love to permissiveness, we'll be upset at God's wrath displayed in the OT record. Our disdain for such a disciplinarian type of love will distract us from the OT testimony that God is a "compassionate and gracious God, slow to anger, abounding in love and faithfulness, maintaining love to thousands, and forgiving wickedness, rebellion and sin" (Exodus 34:6–7; see also Psalm 86:15).

God's Justice and Holiness

God's love is not as anemic as we make it out to be. It is a full-bodied love enriched by all of God's other attributes—such as his holiness and his sense of justice, which compel him to abhor evil. Have you ever considered that justice is a necessary component of true love? Perhaps you've heard of "justice" defined in this manner: Justice is going to the bottom of a cliff to care for those who were pushed off of it, then climbing back to the top to stop whoever was doing the pushing.

God's sense of justice and his holiness are undervalued components of his love. All would agree that the best way to love those who had been pushed off the cliff is to meet them in their need, have compassion for their pain, bandage their wounds, and restore them to health. But it can't stop there. Anyone who has actually been pushed off a cliff would likely agree that loving the cliff-fallen also includes returning to the scene of the crime and holding accountable (stopping, and even punishing) whoever is guilty of pushing them in the first place. Love is not just caring for the injured; it's preventing the injury in the first place, and then dealing with the perpetrators with a vengeance if appropriate.

For those who have never been pushed off a cliff, a more commonplace analogy might be helpful. Suppose you are the parent of an energetic two-year-old daughter. Although she is only a toddler, she can do much more than toddle. She can sprint. To help her expend her energy (so you can preserve your sanity), you take her for a walk around the block. But she is not content to walk. She bolts out the door to explore what for her is uncharted territory.

As you both approach the street intersection, her wonder of the unknown only increases. She proceeds across the curb with unbridled enthusiasm. You quickly squeeze her hand with a vise-like grasp and nearly yank her shoulder out of its socket as you pull her back onto the safety of the sidewalk. You issue a stern proclamation: "No running into the street!"

Are you being too harsh to this young one, who didn't think she was doing anything wrong? Absolutely not! You are simply imposing limitations to her behavior *for her own safety and well-being*. And the next day when the scenario repeats itself and your daughter darts into the street once again, you pull her back again, but this time you give her tiny heinie a measured swat, just firm enough to get her attention and instill a Pavlovian-like reaction the next time she considers crossing the curb. Are you a horrible parent? Quite the contrary. Your love has included discipline *to rescue your daughter from endangering herself*.

And so it is with God, only much more so. Much more than we do, he understands that sin can ensnare us and lead to our destruction. As he deems appropriate, he may unleash the full fury of his wrath against evil, and he may bring discipline in our lives to yank us back onto the curb to avoid an oncoming collision with sin. His love for us is that deep.

Paul (a NT author) quotes Moses (an OT author) when he writes about God's love mixed with his holiness and justice: "Do not take revenge, my dear friends, but leave room for God's wrath, for it is written: 'It is mine to avenge; I will repay,' says the Lord" (Romans 12:19). Paul goes on to poignantly instruct followers of God in Christ to care for their enemies and to fight evil with good.

But God, because he is holy, can exact punishment where it must be exacted, and thankfully for you and us, that punishment was poured out on Christ, who took on himself the sin of the world though he was totally innocent (Isaiah 53:10; John 1:29).

Instead of God's wrath being poured out against us in the OT form of plagues or foreign armies because of our sin, Christ took the heat. Jesus took the punishment that we deserved. And in so doing he satisfied God's holy and justifiable wrath against our sin and evil. The thing that disappeared from the Old Testament to the New Testament was not God's wrath; it was our role in receiving it. God—in the greatest act of love and grace—took it on himself to protect us. And that is good news. That is *the* good news.

QUESTIONS FOR REFLECTION AND DISCUSSION

- Can you think of lyrics from a contemporary song that give a description of love?
- Can you think of a verse that reflects a biblical view of love?
- Describe some of the dynamics of God's love for us.
- How does our love for God compare to his love for us?

Don't Let the Two Testaments Obscure the One Story

The Bible is God's story, and he could have written it in any fashion. So instead of assuming that the two Testaments are at odds with each other (even though it may appear that way to a casual observer), let's carefully read the Bible in search of a cohesive message. If the OT seems different from the NT, let's not accuse God of having two personalities, or at the very least, of having poor editing skills. Maybe we are reading the Bible as if it were two separate novels—OT and NT—instead of one story.

The Wizard of Oz is a book we haven't read, so we'll just refer to the movie. Suppose one person watched only the Kansas part of the movie, and another person watched only the Emerald City part of the movie. When they discuss the movie clips they each respectively viewed, they won't believe they were watching the same film. Yet in reality, it takes both parts to present the truly great story. And so it is with the Bible:

- The OT can seem as dry and dusty as Kansas. From time to time it is action-packed like a tornado. But at times, reading through it can seem, well . . . black and white.
- In contrast, the NT grabs most readers with the excitement and vitality of the Emerald City. It presents a much more exciting narrative that the reader can envision in Technicolor.

Together the OT and the NT present one singular, compelling story. The overarching metanarrative is God's relentless pursuit of reconciliation with a humanity that rebelled against and rejected him. It takes both the OT and the NT to fully explain the magnitude and magnificence of God's plan:

- The OT speaks of God's law (that there must be a sacrifice as the penalty for sin). The NT presents Jesus as the sacrificial lamb that was so prominent in the OT.
- The OT predicts the coming of the Messiah who will be mankind's Savior. The NT proclaims that Jesus is the Messiah who fulfilled the more than three hundred prophecies in the OT.
- The OT declares that God's relationship with humanity was severed by Adam's sin. The NT promises that a relationship with God can be restored by Jesus.
- The OT looks forward to the cross. The NT focuses on the cross, and looks forward to eternity.
- The story that the OT starts, the NT completes.

The Bible is a fascinating and engaging story, but you have to read both Testaments to experience its fullness and to appreciate the full picture of a God who is at once holy, loving, merciful, and just.

QUESTIONS FOR REFLECTION AND DISCUSSION

- Has your view of God changed after reading this chapter? How so?
- What is the downside of a Christ-follower avoiding the OT?
- What are the advantages of reading both Testaments?

7

Is Jesus God?

Introduction

A few years ago, we (Bruce and Stan) were doing research for a book about science, specifically about how the world began. Our goal was to see if science and the Bible were compatible, so we decided to interview some well-known scientists to see what they said about how the universe came into existence. We traveled to the University of California at Berkeley and talked with a world-renowned astrophysicist who was known for leading the team that developed the Cosmic Background Explorer (COBE), a satellite that was the first to measure the heat (which is still radiating outward in space) from the first creation event, commonly known as the Big Bang.

As far as we knew, this eminent scientist did not believe in God (although he said the findings of the COBE satellite raised serious questions about the scientific theory that the universe began on its own). And never during our interviews did we reveal that we are followers of Jesus. Yet as our conversation came to a close and we were literally on our way out the door, the scientist stopped us with two startling questions.

"Can you help me with something?" he asked. "Why is it that someone can live a really bad life, and then on his death bed say he believes in Jesus, and he goes to heaven? And why is it that someone else can live a really good life, but die without believing in Jesus, and go to hell? I've never understood that."

■ ■ ■

Questions about Jesus have been around since he first appeared on the earth. Jesus was announced by the prophets in the Old Testament as *Immanuel*, God with us (Isaiah 7:14). When the holy night of his birth finally arrived, the angelic host proclaimed that the *Messiah*, the deliverer, had come (Luke 2:11). As instructed by an angel of the Lord, Joseph and Mary gave him the name *Jesus*, "because he will save his people from their sins" (Matthew 1:21).

Jesus is all of this—God with us, Messiah, Savior—but that's not all. The Bible claims, and Jesus said so himself, that he is also God in human form.

Perhaps our scientist friend didn't realize it, but his question about the ability of Jesus to save people was a question about the divinity of Jesus. Because if Jesus was just a man, a wise teacher, a good role model, then believing in him wouldn't make any difference. But if he is much more than that—if he is who he said he was—then believing in him makes all the difference in the world.

In fact, our assumption to this point in the book is that Jesus is God, but we haven't yet taken time to explain why we believe that. That's what we want to do now, for one simple reason: When you are searching for truth about God, you have to deal with Jesus as God, because that is who he claimed to be.

Where Do We Go for Answers?

No credible historian doubts the existence of a historical Jesus. He lived at the beginning of the first century AD. Except for a brief detour to Egypt when he was an infant, he spent his life in Israel, in an approximate range of seventy-five miles from the Sea of Galilee in the north to Jerusalem in the south. Those are well-accepted facts no one seriously disputes.

The controversy that has swirled about him for two thousand years relates to *who* or *what* he was; it has never been about the reality of his physical presence on earth. The leading historian during the early Roman Empire was Flavius Josephus. In AD 93, Josephus published a lengthy history of the Jews called *Jewish Antiquities*. In the section covering the period when the Jews of Judea were governed by the Roman procurator Pontius Pilate, Josephus wrote:

> About this time there lived Jesus, a wise man, if indeed one ought to call him a man. For he was one who performed surprising deeds and was a teacher of such people as accept the truth gladly. He won over many Jews and many of the Greeks. He was the Messiah. And when, upon the accusation of the principal men among us, Pilate had condemned him to a cross, those who had first come to love him did not cease. He appeared to them spending a third day restored to life, for the prophets of God had foretold these things and a thousand other marvels about him. And the tribe of the Christians, so called after him, has still to this day not disappeared.[1]

As with most statements about Jesus Christ, this snippet from the writings of Josephus also has its proponents and detractors. So for purposes of this chapter, the Bible will be our sole source of reference material because, well, the Bible includes the most comprehensive historical record about the life of Jesus. Skeptics discredit the Bible simply because it's a religious book, but is that a legitimate complaint? We don't think so. The Bible includes firsthand, eyewitness reports by those who knew Jesus and traveled with him.

We'll be taking the Bible's statements about Jesus at face value, but that doesn't mean you have to. As you'll soon see, the unique life of Jesus Christ is totally amazing and borders on the unbelievable. If you find it a little bit implausible that this unemployed son of a Jewish carpenter was God, you won't be the first.

QUESTIONS FOR REFLECTION AND DISCUSSION

- How do you feel about using the Bible as the only source of information about Jesus?
- Do you think the four mini-biographies of Jesus (the gospels of Matthew, Mark, Luke, and John) are objective in their reporting, or are they biased propaganda?
- Why do you think so many people are skeptical about who Jesus was and what he did?

Let's Start With a Clean Slate

As we begin to build a profile of Jesus—leading to an examination of whether he is God—let's dump all of our preconceived notions about him that may or may not be correct. During our lifetimes, whether we are Christians or not, we all form a mental picture of Jesus. This tendency usually results in his looking exactly how we want him to look, but not necessarily being an accurate depiction of who he is. We might even have several different, contrasting images of him. Depending on our daily circumstances, we can conveniently refer to the image of Jesus that we think best suits our current situation. In our book *I Can't See God Because I'm in the Way*, we shared some of our previously held (and misconceived) mental images of Jesus:

- *Bobblehead Jesus*—He sits on a shelf, like a good luck charm, and we can think about him if we are having an emotional day and need a lighthearted lift.
- *Baby Jesus*—This mental image is not reserved for Christmastime. This is the most non-confrontational way to think

126

about him. He is sweet and innocent, and totally unaware of what we're doing (and we'd like to keep it that way).

- *Soft and Tender Jesus*—Not to be confused with Baby Jesus, this is a full-grown version that is always compassionate and caring, particularly when we've blown it. We opt for this mental image when we need forgiveness and mercy, so we are looking for a Jesus with these attributes but who is totally void of any sense of justice and judgment.

- *Action-figure Jesus*—An alter ego to Soft and Tender Jesus, this is the Jesus who picks up our 9-1-1 prayer and can do something about it. We resort to him only when we're in a tight spot.[2]

While these images differ, they all have one thing in common: Each has stripped Christ of the totality of his uniqueness, and thus his divinity. Whether we do so consciously or subconsciously, when we adopt such simplistic notions of Jesus, we make him a god but don't equate him with the one true God.

We admit that not everyone reduces Jesus to the caricatures listed above. But even if our mental hard drive lacks such misguided notions of Jesus, we are still likely to have some scaled-down concept of him in our imagination. Bible scholar and professor Scot McKnight suggests three categories into which Jesus' identity is most often reduced. And although each "presents something about Jesus that is vital for our understanding," all are "inadequate for describing the whole of Jesus' life and mission."[3] Here are the descriptive categories into which even well-intentioned followers of Christ might put Jesus:

- *Jesus the Sage*—This Jesus is a wise and articulate teacher. He dispenses his popular and countercultural advice with pithy sayings that pack an incisive punch. He's a good teacher, but nothing more.

- *Jesus the Religious Genius*—This Jesus is so deeply religious that his experiences of God and faith are far more significant,

deep, and authentic than other observers of religion. And
he's a bit obsessed with the end of time. He's a religious
fanatic, but nothing more.

- *Jesus the Social Revolutionary*—This Jesus became the leader
of a powerful social and political movement when his messages of equality and peace disrupted Roman and Jewish
society. He's a social reformer, but nothing more.[4]

Besides our own selfish desires for the type of Jesus we want
(instead of how he really is), there is another pressure at work
to mold our thoughts of him. This subconscious tension may be
particularly compelling to Christians who want their Jesus to be
socially acceptable. We are referring to the desire for a "politically
correct" Jesus: a Jesus who will be acceptable to our contemporary
twenty-first-century culture; a Jesus who won't ruffle any feathers;
a Jesus who will be moral, but not with an antiquated morality;
and a Jesus who has a sense of social justice, but who won't put
demands upon us to participate in solutions beyond the limits of
our own convenience.

After all, Christians are called to spread the good news of Jesus
Christ. The spreading will be much easier with a Jesus who is popular with the masses. But theologian William Lane Craig explains
why our desire to make Jesus politically (or personally) correct is
faulty thinking on our part:

> If you insist on being politically correct, then somehow you've got
> to get Jesus out of the way. For his radical, personal claims to be
> the unique Son of God, the absolute revelation of God the Father,
> the sole mediator between God and man, are frankly embarrassing
> and offensive to the politically correct mindset.[5]

The overriding problem with all of these variant and customized
views of Jesus is simple: *They present a Jesus who doesn't exist.*
These characteristics may reflect *the Jesus we want*, but they do
not define *the Jesus who is*. If that's the case, we need to realign
our thinking by putting personal preferences and self-conceived

notions of Jesus aside in favor of finding a biblically based description of him.

QUESTIONS FOR REFLECTION AND DISCUSSION

- What do you think of Jesus?
- Which of the above versions of Jesus is most attractive to you? Why?
- What does your customized Jesus look like? (We've all done this, so don't feel bad. Be honest!) What happens to Jesus when we do this?
- Are there detriments to relying on a version of Jesus that is something different from the real deal?

Meet the Real Jesus: A Life Like No Other

To say that Jesus lived a unique life is an understatement. To a certain extent, there is an aspect of every human life that is unique (beginning with fingerprints), but there is considerable overlap among us all when it comes to life events and circumstances. The life of Christ, however, encompasses a myriad of highlights that no other human could ever replicate. Here are a few of the most obvious ones:

- *Jesus was born of a virgin* (Luke 1:26–38). That's as unique as it gets, and it means that Jesus had a parentage that was both human (his mother) and divine (the Holy Spirit).
- *Jesus lived a fully human but perfect life.* Jesus "had no sin" (2 Corinthians 5:21). He's the only person in human history who could make this claim.
- *Jesus performed miracles.* The Bible records about thirty-five miracles performed by Jesus. These were supernatural acts that do not have natural explanations.
- *Jesus died by crucifixion* (Matthew 27:32–56). Okay, crucifixion in the Roman Empire wasn't unique. Many others were

crucified. But the circumstances of his crucifixion set Jesus apart. While crucifixion was reserved for the most heinous of criminals, the Roman authority who issued the death sentence declared that there was no basis for a criminal charge against Jesus (John 19:6). Jesus didn't resist his execution, because his death was necessary for the salvation of mankind (Hebrews 2:5–18).

- *Jesus came back from the dead* (John 20–21). Though his disciples didn't believe that Jesus would rise from the dead, they witnessed the resurrected Christ firsthand. They weren't the only ones. More than five hundred people saw Jesus in the forty days between his resurrection and his ascension (1 Corinthians 15:6).

- *Jesus ascended into heaven* (Acts 1:1–11). In the presence of a group of his followers, Jesus ascended from earth into the sky. When they lost sight of him in the clouds, two men in white garments appeared among them and said, "This same Jesus, who has been taken from you into heaven, will come back in the same way you have seen him go into heaven" (v. 11).

The four biographers who gave us these reports in the Gospels had a specific purpose for doing so (and it wasn't for royalties from sales of the Bible). As John stated it:

> Jesus performed many other signs in the presence of his disciples, which are not recorded in this book. But these are written that you may believe that Jesus is the Messiah, the Son of God, and that by believing you may have life in his name.
>
> John 20:30–31

QUESTIONS FOR REFLECTION AND DISCUSSION

- Do you find the weight of evidence as presented by the gospel writers to be persuasive that Jesus was God?
- Why does it matter?

Meet the Real Jesus: What God Said About Jesus

It might be helpful to get God's opinion on the question of whether Jesus is God. That isn't as difficult as you might suspect, because God hasn't been silent on this issue.

- *God spoke about Jesus when Jesus was baptized.* Here's the scene as reported in Mark 1:9–11:

  At that time Jesus came from Nazareth in Galilee and was baptized by John in the Jordan. Just as Jesus was coming up out of the water, he saw heaven being torn open and the Spirit descending on him like a dove. And a voice came from heaven: "You are my Son, whom I love; with you I am well pleased."

- *God spoke about Jesus at the transfiguration.* From Matthew 17:1–5 in *The Message* translation, we have this report:

  Jesus took Peter and the brothers, James and John, and led them up a high mountain. His appearance changed from the inside out, right before their eyes. Sunlight poured from his face. His clothes were filled with light. Then they realized that Moses and Elijah were also there in deep conversation with him. Peter broke in, "Master, this is a great moment! What would you think if I built three memorials here on the mountain—one for you, one for Moses, one for Elijah? While he was going on like this, babbling, a light-radiant cloud enveloped them, and sounding from deep in the cloud a voice: "This is my Son, marked by my love, focus of my delight. Listen to him."

- *God inspired the apostle Paul to write about God's opinion of Jesus.* As we discussed in chapter 4, the writers of the Bible were inspired by God to communicate his message. They wrote as God prompted them. So when the apostle

Paul penned what God thinks and feels, he had received that message firsthand. On the subject of whether Jesus is God, here is how Paul reported God's answer:

> Christ is the visible image of the invisible God. He existed before anything was created and is supreme over all creation. . . . He [Jesus] existed before anything else, and he holds all creation together. . . . For God in all his fullness was pleased to live in Christ, and through him God reconciled everything to himself.
>
> Colossians 1:15, 17, 19–20 NLT

QUESTIONS FOR REFLECTION AND DISCUSSION

- Imagine that you are on the shore of the Jordan River when Jesus was being baptized. Now, reread Matthew 17:1-5. You are an eyewitness to this event. Would it have impacted your opinion of whether Jesus was God?

- Now, approximately two thousand years later, does this even influence your opinion of who Jesus is?

Meet the Real Jesus: Jesus Knows He Is What We Need From God

In the fourth gospel, John records seven "I am" statements made by Jesus. These statements show two things: First, Jesus is fully self-aware. He knows (and articulates) who he is, so we don't have to make stuff up about him. Second, they show that he also knows what we need from God. So in his "I am" statements, he declares both his identity as God and his knowledge that he is everything we truly need.

- *Jesus is the Bread of Life.* He satisfies our spiritual hunger and thirst.

"I am the bread of life. Whoever comes to me will never go hungry, and whoever believes in me will never be thirsty."

John 6:35

- *Jesus is the Light of the World*. He brings spiritual light and understanding into our spiritual darkness.

    "I am the light of the world. Whoever follows me will never walk in darkness, but will have the light of life."

    John 8:12

- *Jesus is the gate*. He is the key to spiritual fulfillment and eternal salvation.

    "I am the gate; whoever enters through me will be saved. They will come in and go out, and find pasture."

    John 10:9

- *Jesus is the Good Shepherd*. He is our guide and protector, caring and providing for our every need.

    "I am the good shepherd. The good shepherd lays down his life for the sheep."

    John 10:11

- *Jesus is the resurrection and the life*. As our resurrection and life, there is eternal life in Jesus; our physical death is not to be feared.

    "I am the resurrection and the life. The one who believes in me will live, even though they die."

    John 11:25

- *Jesus is the way, the truth, and the life*. Jesus is our only conduit for connecting with God.

    "I am the way and the truth and the life. No one comes to the Father except through me."

    John 14:6

133

- *Jesus is the Vine.* After identifying himself as the vine, Jesus called us the "branches" (John 15:5). It is through the vine that the branches receive life and sustenance.

> "I am the true vine, and my Father is the gardener."
>
> John 15:1

Deep down (but not all that deep, much of the time), most of us long to be spiritually satisfied, to walk in light rather than darkness, to know the way to spiritual fulfillment, and to establish an intimate relationship with God. We desire to know the source of a true, good, and meaningful life. In these seven identity statements, Jesus not only claims to be and do what God is and does but also identifies himself to be who and what we are searching for.

QUESTIONS FOR REFLECTION AND DISCUSSION

- Do these "I am" statements answer the question "Does God care about me and my problems?" Why or why not?
- Do any of these statements give you assurance that Jesus is qualified to be your guide for life? If so, which ones?

Meet the Real Jesus: What Jesus Said About Himself

Basis question: Did Jesus ever publicly announce that he was God?

Lawyer-like answer: Well, it depends on what you mean by "announce."

Simple explanation: Nowhere in the Bible does it report that Jesus said the precise words "I am God." But he clearly conveyed that message in many ways on many occasions. Below are examples of how the "I am God" meaning was clearly and boldly communicated through two often-repeated statements in the New Testament.

Jesus said: "The Father and I are one"

The story is told in John 10:30–39. Jesus was in the temple, answering questions about whether he was the Messiah. As usual, members of the Jewish religious elite were well represented in the crowd. In his discourse, Jesus boldly stated, "I and the Father are one" (v. 30). While the ears of a twenty-first-century audience might not hear "I am God" in those words, that is exactly what the Jews in the temple understood Jesus to be saying. In fact, they immediately tried to stone him. As he was about to be pummeled with rocks, Jesus asked why they were so suddenly and vehemently upset with him. Their response revealed the transparency of his "I and the Father are one" statement: They answered that they were stoning him "for blasphemy, because you, a mere man, claim to be God" (v. 33).

Yes, Jesus claimed to be God, and this confrontation with the Jewish establishment provides rock-solid proof. [Spoiler alert: They didn't get a chance to stone him, although they tried. He managed to "escape their grasp" (v. 39). Another example of when supernatural powers come in handy.]

Jesus affirmed: "I am the Son of God"

There is no biblical record that Jesus ever mouthed the words "I am the Son of God." But other people said it, he never denied it, and sometimes he affirmed it. Here are some of the revealing passages:

- They all asked, "Are you then the Son of God?" He replied, "You say that I am" (Luke 22:70).
- "But what about you?" [Jesus] asked. "Who do you say I am?" Simon Peter answered, "You are the Messiah, the Son of the living God." Jesus replied, "Blessed are you, Simon son of Jonah, for this was not revealed to you by flesh and blood, but by my Father in heaven" (Matthew 16:15–17).

135

- The high priest said to him, "I charge you under oath by the living God: Tell us if you are the Messiah, the Son of God." "You have said so," Jesus replied (Matthew 26:63–64).

The "Son of God" references may seem like no big deal today; any whack job with a microphone might claim he is the Son of God. But in first-century Israel, to announce you were another's son was to announce you were his equal—in status, responsibility, power, and authority. A son, particularly the firstborn son, and his father were deemed to be alike in every significant cultural way. By claiming to be the Son of God, Jesus claimed to be equal to God in nature. This is why he could accept the title of "Son of God." And it's why the Jewish religious leaders said to crucify him (John 19:6).

So Is Jesus God?

By the time of his ascension, Jesus had many followers who accepted him as God. However, the concept that "Jesus is God" infuriated the religious leaders of his day. In attempts to discredit him, they attacked his mental status, alleging he was demon-possessed and insane (John 10:20 ESV).

It is now twenty centuries later. It is estimated that approximately 2.2 billion people identify as followers of Christ. That's a big number, but with a world population of 7 billion, it is obvious that many reject (or ignore) the "Jesus is God" position. Interestingly, the only logical conclusion for contemporary dissenters is similar to criticism from the first century: Jesus must have been messed up mentally.

C. S. Lewis confronted the attempts to discredit the divinity of Jesus with his famous "poached egg" argument. He offered three viewpoints. Either Jesus was lying about his identity, he was deranged, or he was indeed who he said he was. It's one of the three. It's not possible for him to be anything else—such as a great moral teacher—because he never claimed to be that. He claimed to be God. So you have to deal with that claim in evaluating Jesus. In his classic *Mere Christianity*, Lewis wrote it this way:

> A man who was merely a man and said the sort of things Jesus said would not be a great moral teacher. He would either be a lunatic—on a level with the man who says he is a poached egg—or else he would be the Devil of Hell. You must make your choice. Either this man was, and is, the Son of God: or else a madman or something worse.[6]

We've wrestled with the "Is Jesus God?" question from several perspectives. Let's conclude our analysis from the logical perspective suggested by C. S. Lewis. We'll ask the three questions Lewis poses for assessing the true nature of Jesus.

1. Was Jesus crazy?

More politely put, was Jesus mentally unstable? Was his assertion to be God the product of a chemical imbalance or other mental deficiency? The answer from Dr. Gary R. Collins—a clinical psychologist and chair of the psychology division at Trinity Evangelical Divinity School—is a succinct no. Dr. Collins explains his certainty with a variety of psychological proofs:

- Jesus never demonstrated inappropriate emotions.
- Jesus wasn't paranoid.
- Jesus spoke clearly, powerfully, and eloquently.
- His relationships with those closest to him were healthy.
- Even though he was surrounded by enormous crowds of people who hung on his every word, he didn't have a "bloated ego."
- He understood human nature.[7]

According to Collins's assessment, these are not the actions of a raving lunatic. The Gospels reveal the actions and words of someone who was mentally and emotionally healthy.

2. Was Jesus a liar?

If Jesus was a liar, his followers didn't get the message. True, some people will die for a lie, but only because they believe—without doubt—that it's true. People don't die for something they *know* is a lie.

All but one of the disciples of Jesus died for him (John, the exception, was exiled when the authorities were unsuccessful at killing him). Peter, James, John, and the rest were convinced that Jesus was who he said he was—God in the flesh—because they were eyewitnesses to the life, teachings, healings, death, and resurrection of Jesus. Here's what Peter wrote:

> For we did not follow cleverly devised stories when we told you about the coming of our Lord Jesus Christ in power, but we were eyewitnesses of his majesty.
>
> 2 Peter 1:16

The disciples knew Jesus intimately. If he was lying, wouldn't they have abandoned him? Was it worth the risk of death to hide behind a lie? Or is it easier to understand that Jesus transformed these ordinary men into bold and persuasive witnesses to the reality and power of Christ?

3. Is Jesus God?

Anyone can make the claim. But is there evidence that Jesus actually is God? Here are a handful of things to consider:

- Jesus performed miracles.
- Jesus forgave sins.
- Jesus had supernatural attributes.
- Jesus rose from the dead.

Many have found Jesus to be God. Many don't agree. In the end, it is a personal decision. But it's not a decision based on pure speculation or blind faith.

- Does the use of rational arguments (like that of C. S. Lewis) bolster your belief that Jesus is God? Why or why not?
- How would you respond to someone who was convinced Jesus was nothing more than a wise teacher who had a Messiah complex? Read 2 Peter 1:16 again.
- How willing are you to trust the eyewitness accounts of the disciples of Jesus? Is there any reason why the followers of Jesus were not telling the truth about what they saw?
- Are you at a disadvantage because you can't experience Jesus in person? Why or why not? How important is it to you that Jesus rose from the dead? Read 1 Corinthians 15:17.

God's Rescue Plan

When we study theology, one of our favorite questions to pose is this: Why does it matter? We can talk about lofty theological realities (the explanation of the Trinity) or biblical trivialities (Adam and Eve are the only humans who didn't have belly buttons), but if these discussions don't hit the ground of everyday life, what good are they? The same is true here. So we need to ask this important question: Why does it matter whether Jesus was God in the flesh?

The short answer is this: Because according to the Bible, Jesus is God's plan for our rescue and redemption.

Here's how God's rescue plan unfolded in real time:

- Humanity's great rebellion against God first occurred in the garden of Eden, and it severed the intimate relationship between God and his people (Genesis 3).
- When hope seemingly died, God set into motion his rescue plan for all humanity. It was a plan centered in Jesus Christ (Ephesians 1:9–10).
- God spoke through the prophets with a message full of hope: God would send a Messiah, the anointed King, who would

139

be a suffering servant to carry the sorrows of God's people and ultimately be a Savior for the human race (Isaiah 53).

- Jesus, the Son of God, came to earth as the Messiah. He lived a perfect and sinless life, by which his death was sufficient to pay the penalty for all the sins of humanity (Romans 3:23).

- All people—Jews and Gentiles, slave and free, men and women—can benefit from God's rescue plan by turning their lives over to Jesus Christ. Through his sacrifice, those who believe in him can be reconciled into an intimate relationship with God (Acts 2:21; Romans 10:13).

The good news of the gospel is not that Jesus' followers get to go to heaven. The good news of the gospel is not that the church is mobilized by God to help heal the world. The good news is this: Jesus of Nazareth, who was crucified and buried and rose from the dead, is Lord of all. We have a God who can empathize with us: He knows what it is like to live on earth and suffer the frailties and troubles of the human condition.

Because Jesus is Lord of all, those who surrender their lives to him do not need to fear death; they will live eternally with him. And because Jesus is Lord of all, we do not need to wonder about our mission on earth; we can follow the Lord, who has called us to care for and help heal this hurting world. Jesus the Lord rescues us from death and from a useless life.

QUESTIONS FOR REFLECTION AND DISCUSSION

- What do you think of God's rescue plan?
- Why was such a plan necessary? Why did it take so long to unfold?
- How did God's people miss the clues? How do we miss the clues today?
- Describe a time when you felt the authority of Jesus. How about his empathy?

For some people, the "Is Jesus God" question is a no-brainer; they can easily reach a yes or no conclusion. Others spend a life-time wrestling with the issue. The tipping point is belief: Do you *believe* in Jesus?

When the apostle Paul was in prison (Acts 16:16–31), the guard asked him, "What must I do to be saved?" Paul responded with an answer that is easily understood and applicable to us all: "Believe in the Lord Jesus Christ, and you will be saved." (He didn't use the phrase "God's rescue plan," but that is what he was referring to.)

There are different levels of belief, and it's important that you know the difference. If you believe that Jesus lived and died and rose from the dead, then you have a faith based on *knowing who Jesus is*. If you believe that Jesus is the Son of God and the only way to establish a relationship with God, then your faith is based on *agreeing with what Jesus said*. Essentially, you move from be-lieving *in* Jesus to *believing* Jesus.

The further step of belief is to actually step out in faith and put your whole life, without conditions, into the hands of Jesus. You believe him for your salvation. This is when your belief is complete, because you don't just *know about* Jesus; you don't just *agree with* Jesus; you make a decision to *receive his grace and follow him fully*.

QUESTIONS FOR REFLECTION AND DISCUSSION

- As C. S. Lewis observed, Jesus doesn't leave any other option. Either he's a lunatic or a liar, or he's Lord. If Jesus was telling the truth and he is God, then it is incumbent upon each of us to offer some kind of response. What is your response?

- It's okay if you're not ready. Keep reading. Stay with us. If you have responded already, how has this chapter changed the way you view Jesus?

8

Why Do Christians Say Jesus Is the Only Way to God?

Introduction

Hillary has traveled the world since early in her college career. She was a Spanish and international business major, and she took every opportunity presented to her to visit new countries, take a semester abroad, and immerse herself in Spanish-speaking countries. In college she shared notes with Japanese students, studied with Muslim students whose families still lived in Iran, and hung out in the student center with fellow Americans as well as South Americans. She recently graduated and plans to work for a year to save enough money to live in Argentina for an additional year of Spanish immersion and study.

Hillary was raised in a family that she describes as "faith neutral—not against, but not for, either." It was only after starting college that Hillary began to seriously interact with people who held strong religious beliefs, most of them from vastly different cultural backgrounds. A recent conversation with Hillary about the ongoing strife amid Islamic countries led to a discussion of Christianity. The topic was as foreign to her as the subject of Islam would be to most American Christians. She visibly bristled a bit when she heard that Christians believe the Bible teaches that a person must accept Jesus Christ as Savior in order to know and experience God.

"Most of the faith-sensitive people I know are Muslim," she explained. "Others haven't joined a faith yet, but they are on a journey to find God. These are devout friends, making a genuine attempt to please their God or to find God." Then she asked a question that revealed the heart of her curiosity: "So why do Christians say Jesus is the only way to God?"

■ ■ ■

Christians live in the world with everyone else. It is a world that is becoming increasingly politically correct, which sometimes makes Christians feel like a persecuted minority because some of their beliefs are often viewed as being politically *incorrect*. Christians are fully aware that the doctrines of their faith put them at odds with cultural expectations. Those doctrines include ones that Christians can't always adequately explain, and which the rest of society can't quite understand. Hillary's question presents a prime example.

For a Christian, "Jesus is the only way to God" is a foundational doctrine. It is a linchpin of the Christian faith. But to a non-Christian ear, the mere utterance of that principle grates against the hearer's sensitivities. It shouts of absolutism. It conveys arrogance. It implies exclusivity (and concomitant discrimination). Bottom line: It just seems downright unfair that there is only one way to God.

Hillary's question deserves thoughtful analysis. What follows may not change anyone's opinion. But we think there is an explanation that will satisfy those who share Hillary's question, and it may even help Christians explain their position without the shock and awe that often accompanies it.

- How does Hillary's question sit with you?
- Does the thought of Jesus being the only way to God make you uncomfortable, are you fine with it, or are you undecided?
- Can you understand why non-Christians like Hillary might cringe when they hear it?
- Can you speculate why it would make someone uneasy?

Religious Pluralism: Can One Religion Claim It Is the "True" Way?

Hillary's question is the battle line between the opposing religious worldviews of Christianity and religious pluralism. We'll defer a discussion of the tenets of Christianity to later in the chapter because we want to begin with the ideology of religious pluralism suggested by Hillary's question. Religious pluralism is becoming a more prevalent philosophy in our culture, but we need a definition deeper than "all religions are basically the same." For a source that isn't biased in favor of Christianity, let's turn to Wikipedia, where *religious pluralism* is defined as "an attitude or policy regarding the diversity of religious belief systems co-existing in society."[1] It is a term that encompasses . . .

1. A worldview in which "one's religion is not the sole and exclusive source of truth, and thus the acknowledgement that at least some truths and true values exist in other religions."[2]
2. The belief that "two or more religions with mutually exclusive truth claims are equally valid."[3]
3. A view that "exclusive claims of different religions turn out, upon closer examination, to be variations of universal truths" that have existed forever.[4]

Christians might squirm just a little over the first definition, but they shouldn't. Truth is not proprietary to Christianity alone.

Other faiths include elements of truth. (The sacred writings of the Jewish faith include what the Christians call the Old Testament. That is a basis for common shared truth.) But Christians will most likely be compelled to argue that the *origin* of *all* truth is from their God. This belief that "all truth is God's truth" dates back to about AD 400, when theologian Augustine of Hippo mentioned it in his writings:

> Nay, but let every good and true Christian understand that wherever truth may be found, it belongs to his Master.[5]

The sixteenth-century theologian and reformer John Calvin explained the concept this way:

> All truth is from God; and consequently, if wicked men have said anything that is true and just, we ought not to reject it; for it has come from God.[6]

So Christians are likely to acknowledge that other faiths may have some truth, but they'll insist that all truth finds its genesis in the God of the Bible.

As for definitions #2 and #3, this is where Christian belief doesn't agree. If all truth is from God, then the mutually exclusive "truth" claims of another faith cannot have any validity (#2). If all truth comes from God, and if another faith has a claim that conflicts with God's truth, then the conflicting claim must have come from a source other than God.

Similarly, Christian doctrine will not permit the notion that opposing truth claims of all faiths turn out, in the end, to be variations of an underlying universal truth (#3). This definition is often illustrated with the following story: People of all faiths are climbing a mountain to find god. Each faith takes a different path up the mountain, but they all meet at the top and realize that they have all been worshiping the same god. The illustration fails for Christians. For them, there is only one God who has revealed himself and his teachings in his Word (the Bible). No mountain climbing necessary.

When Hillary reads that Christians reject definitions #2 and #3, she might say, "There they go again, those Christians, thinking they have a lock on the truth." But we shouldn't be too hard on the Christians. Each and every religion would, at the level of its core beliefs, reject definitions #2 and #3. Why? Because along with Christianity, each and every other religion believes that its principles are true, and that opposing claims of other faiths are false.

- As to mutually exclusive truth claims both being valid (definition #2), consider the contrast between Buddhism and Islam. Buddhism doesn't believe in the existence of any god; Islam believes in a personal God that is omnipotent, omniscient, and holy. Buddhism believes that the world is eternal, but people do not have souls, and there is no heaven or hell; Islam believes that people must earn their salvation with God, and that there is a real heaven and hell. With drastic contrasts such as these among the world's religions, the "truths" of all religions cannot all be true. Logic dictates, however, that they could all be false.[7]

- Regarding definition #3 (that all religions are basically the same), consider this: Blending all religions into one amorphous clump might make sense to someone who has no religious faith and knows nothing about the religions of the world. But according to Dr. Craig Hazen, an expert in comparative world religions, scholars aren't keen on agreeing that one God fits all because the doctrinal incompatibilities are so drastic.[8]

It seems that religious pluralism is an acceptable theory for atheists and people who have no religious commitment. But for those who have a strong faith belief (whether Christian or any other religion), the concepts of religious pluralism are nonsensical. This means that the Christian view that "Jesus is the only way to God" is not any more dogmatic or arrogant than a competing doctrine of another religion.

Why Only One Way to God? Does That Seem Fair to You?

Let's set religious pluralism aside. Christianity shouldn't be criticized simply because it claims to be true. All faiths make a claim on being the one true way. But let's look at the very claim of Christianity that raised the one question that troubled Hillary: Jesus is the *only* way to God. To Hillary and many others, it just doesn't seem fair. Why only one way?

We are a society that enjoys having options: a myriad of coffee selections at Starbucks (with even more permutations dependent upon personal preference), more than 31 flavors of ice cream at Baskin-Robbins, over 10,000 varieties of wine grapes in the world, and more cable television shows than any one person can follow in a lifetime. You get the idea. We like having alternatives. So if God is all-knowing, shouldn't he have known that we'd prefer having a few options available for selecting our mode of salvation?

Hillary and others with her question don't seem to complain about Jesus being a way to reach God. They are just uncomfortable with Jesus being the *only* way. There's no margin left for personal freedom. We don't like the idea of being herded down the same road as everyone else. We need options to exercise our own self-expression. To the twenty-first-century mind, in an aspect of life as important as connecting with God, having only one route imposed upon us seems arbitrary and capricious. Bottom line: It doesn't seem fair.

The Disney Diversion

The authors of this book all live in California. We realize that there is a Disney World in Florida, and other Disney theme parks around the world. But for us and our respective lineage, all things Disney emanate from Disneyland in Anaheim, California.

Disneyland's current average daily attendance is about 46,000 people. Since Disneyland opened in 1955, more than 650 million guests have entered the park. Every single one of them has entered through the one and only entrance, which opens onto the south end of Main Street, U.S.A. That's a lot of people to go through one entrance. There are lots of turnstiles to handle those 46,000 each day, but all are lined up at the one entrance.

Hmm, now that we think about it, in all our visits, we've never heard anyone complain about having only one entrance. Maybe that's because all the visitors are thrilled at the prospect of entering the "Happiest Place on Earth." A little waiting, a little shoving, a little sweating, only one entrance . . . these are minor inconveniences compared with the adventure that awaits them. Sure, Walt could have designed the park differently, with ancillary entrances adjoining Tomorrowland on the east side, and another at what is now Critter Country on the west. But those 46,000 people seem to intuitively understand that Walt knew what was best. He had their enjoyment in mind, so they trust his judgment and dare not question his providential plan.

Apparently, no one thinks that the solitary entrance into Disneyland is unfair.

Back to "Jesus Is the Only Way to God"— Does It Still Seem Unfair?

We don't need to hammer on the analogy; you get it. But we can't resist. When one considers the reward that awaits us—having a personal, intimate relationship with the almighty God of the universe; having the Holy Spirit alive and active in your life; and being assured of spending eternity with God—who can legitimately complain that there is only one way to attain it?

And, as with Disneyland guests, there's never a complaint from people who have accepted Jesus Christ as their Savior and conduit to God. They don't mind Jesus being the only way to God because a personal relationship with Jesus is the gift of salvation. Eternal life is a side benefit, but being in daily fellowship with Jesus is the real reward.

Our prayer for people who struggle with Hillary's question is that they won't allow the "one way" issue to be an obstacle that prevents them from knowing Jesus. We haven't interviewed all of the millions of Christ-followers currently living on earth, but we know of no Christian who is still troubled by the limited option available for salvation. It's kind of like the people who complain about Christianity being contrary to the secular idea of religious pluralism. The only people who are troubled by Jesus being the only way to God are the ones who have not yet taken that step of connecting with God.

QUESTIONS FOR REFLECTION

- Have you ever been to Disneyland? Did you complain about there being only one entrance? Do you even remember if the entrance was an issue?
- How about Christianity? Does there being only one way to God bother you? Does it seem unfair to you?
- Can you understand why it might strike people who have no faith as being unfair?

Why Only One Way to God? Doesn't It Seem a Little Narrow-Minded and Intolerant?

We are not intending to disrespect Hillary and the sincerity of her question (or *you* if you share her question). It is just the opposite. We realize that sometimes a question (for which there is a rational answer) merely masks a more complicated question. We think that is the case with Hillary's question for many people. They are not *really* complaining that there is only *one* way to God. But they are uncomfortable with the claim that it has to be Jesus (and no one or no way else). Not that they have anything against Jesus, but they are hesitant to make a spiritual commitment to anyone or anything to the exclusion of other people or things. We understand that. These are matters of eternal significance we are dealing with. Many people are intimidated by the thought of picking only Jesus when there are so many other religious choices.

Let's take Hillary's question, but let's crank it up a little. And we'll use the parlance of people who have presented this amped-up question to us. Here is how it usually goes:

> I've heard that Christians believe that Jesus is the only way to find God. Is that true? To me, actually, that seems narrow-minded and awfully intolerant. You are clearly attempting to make your Jesus the exclusive gateway to God. Either "believe in him" or "go to hell." Well, I have difficulty with being a part of any religion that is so bigoted.

Yep, it takes Hillary's question up a notch, doesn't it? Yet it is still a very legitimate question. And it might have been beneath the surface of Hillary's initial inquiry. Maybe she was just too polite to ask what she really felt. But it deserves a thoughtful response because, at first glance, the knee-jerk reaction to the Christian plan of salvation is that it is exclusionary more than inclusionary.

In this section, we'll be reviewing five very important doctrines of the Christian faith. It is necessary to do so because these biblical principles undergird the belief that Jesus is the only way to God. Our particular focus will be on those doctrines that explain that the Christian plan of salvation—centered on Jesus—excludes no one and is open to everyone.

1. Christianity is egalitarian and open to everyone

Christianity would be exclusive if any category of people was excluded, but none are. There are absolutely no prerequisites. With Christianity, it is "come as you are, whoever you are."

Perhaps John 3:16 is the most famous verse in the Bible because it proclaims this message loud and clear:

Verse	Commentary
For God so loved the world	Meaning all of humanity
That he gave his one and only Son,	The gift of salvation by Jesus' death
That whoever	Anyone, without limitation
Believes in him	Jesus (remember, the way to God)
Shall not perish	Salvation comes through Jesus
But have eternal life.	Life with God for eternity

That the love of God extends to all is a common theme woven throughout the Bible. Here is how it is proclaimed in 1 Timothy 2:3–6 (emphasis added), with the extra bonus reference that Jesus plays the pivotal role in bringing salvation to all who desire it:

> This is good, and pleases God our Savior, **who wants all people to be saved** and to come to a knowledge of the truth. For there is one God and one mediator between God and mankind, **the man Christ Jesus, who gave himself as a ransom for all people.**

Similarly, 1 John 2:2 (emphasis added) proclaims God's love for all and Christ's role in salvation:

> He [Jesus Christ] is the **atoning sacrifice for our sins,** and not only for ours but also for the sins **of the whole world.**

2. Christianity is a free gift of God's grace

In Christian lingo, *grace* means unmerited favor. So when Christians speak of God's grace, it means that God's salvation is available to us even though we don't deserve it. And we don't have to pay for it:

> For it is by grace you have been saved, through faith—and this is not from yourselves, it is the gift of God—not by works, so that no one can boast.
>
> Ephesians 2:8–9

Although God's gift of salvation is free to us, it came at a cost—the sacrificial death of Jesus Christ. As Herman W. Gockel (theologian and religious film director) explains, "There will always be the seeming contradiction—that while God's saving grace is always and forever free, it is never, never cheap."[9]

There is nothing you have to do or perform for God's salvation. Many people live with the belief that eternity with God in heaven will be determined by weighing their "good deeds" during their lifetime against the "bad things" they did in life. If the good outweighs the bad, then you go to heaven. If it doesn't, well, then no salvation for you.

Good deeds are nice and have a beneficial effect, but they are meaningless as far as salvation is concerned. Compared with God and his righteousness, any good deed that we can do is worthless. The Bible says it this way:

> All our righteous acts are like filthy rags.
>
> Isaiah 64:6

Because we have a sin nature, there's nothing we can do on our own to earn God's favor. But this is a good thing. We are never caught in the quandary of wondering if we are good enough for God, because the resounding answer is always "No! We aren't good enough for God." No matter how good we are, and no matter how hard we try, we can't meet God's standard of complete and total holiness. But Christ did meet that standard of complete and total holiness, because he was God incarnate. Jesus is the only sinless person who ever lived. So it is through what he has done—not through our own flailing efforts—that we can be saved.

3. You don't even have to be religious

Many people mistakenly believe that God is impressed by and requires religious activities. But the Bible is clear that going to church, praying, and reading the Bible don't earn salvation points for anyone. Such activities might be a factor in spiritual growth, but they don't impress God as a substitute for faith in Jesus Christ.

Many Jewish leaders in Jesus' time taught that observing religious rituals would earn people good standing with God. The Pharisees in particular were expert rule keepers. They developed a system of 613 laws (248 required actions, and 365 prohibited actions), which they followed "religiously." Unfortunately for them, they worshiped their rituals more than they loved God, and Jesus was not impressed. Instead, the Bible teaches that salvation comes through a personal relationship with Christ, not strict adherence to a religious checklist.

> He saved us, not because of righteous things we had done, but because of his mercy.
>
> Titus 3:5

4. You don't have to belong to a special group

Salvation through Christ is color-blind and gender-neutral, and it knows no geographic boundaries. No ethnic group is discriminated against, and no political party is favored. No group or subset of humanity has an inside track with God. We are all outsiders—separated from God by our sin—until we come to Christ.

During the times of the Old Testament, God showed special favor to the Jews, but since the moments of Christ's death and resurrection, salvation through Jesus Christ is available equally to all humankind.

Words like Jewish and non-Jewish, religious and irreligious, insider and outsider, uncivilized and uncouth, slave and free, mean nothing. From now on everyone is defined by Christ, everyone is included in Christ.

Colossians 3:11 THE MESSAGE

5. You are not disqualified by anything in your past

God doesn't ask to see your "permanent file," and he doesn't care about a criminal record. Just as he is not impressed by a résumé, he also is not repulsed by anything shady in your past. And just as we can't earn salvation with good behavior, we aren't excluded from salvation by any bad conduct.

But there are those who plead: "I'm not good enough for God to save me." That is a true statement. No one is. God's holiness demands perfection. None of us is perfect (and the varying degrees of behavior among us don't even register a blip on God's radar). In God's eyes, we are all just a bunch of sinners . . . until we turn to Christ. Then, through Christ's perfection, God can see us as his children.

Yet to all who did receive him, to those who believed in his name, he gave the right to become the children of God—children born not of natural descent, nor of human decision or a husband's will, but born of God.

John 1:12–13

QUESTIONS FOR REFLECTION AND DISCUSSION

- Review the five doctrinal statements you just read. Are any of them new to you? Which one appeals to you the most?
- In some religions, you are required to change in some manner (i.e., "clean up your act") before you are considered worthy to begin. Can you explain why there are no prerequisites of any kind with Christianity?

Jesus Summed It All Up

For those who follow Christ, God's love extends to all, and his plan of salvation is open to all, with no prerequisites other than belief in Jesus. No narrow-mindedness, no exclusivity, no discrimination, no upfront payment or good deeds required. No other faith makes this offer.

Christians who enjoy God's salvation know that it is all by and through the work of Christ. For them it is not open for debate whether Jesus is the only way to God. From their own personal experience and from pages of the Bible, God speaks clearly and firmly about these points:

- God exists, and he is the God of the Bible.

  > I am the Lord, and there is no other; apart from me there is no God.
  >
  > Isaiah 45:5

- Jesus, the Son of God, is God himself.

  > "Anyone who has seen me has seen the Father. . . . Believe me when I say that I am in the Father and the Father is in me."
  >
  > John 14:9, 11

- Jesus, the Son of God who was God himself, taught that he was the way through which humanity can connect with God.

  > "I am the way and the truth and the life. No one comes to the Father except through me."
  >
  > John 14:6

Christians should respect the right of others to hold different opinions, but the foregoing discussion hopefully makes it clear why Christians are unapologetic about acknowledging Jesus as the only way to God.

And All That Is Required of You Is Belief

Your belief that Jesus Christ paid the penalty for your sin is all that is required on your part for salvation. Once, when the apostle Paul was in jail, he was asked by the guard what is necessary to be saved. Paul's answer was profoundly simple:

> Believe in the Lord Jesus, and you will be saved.
>
> Acts 16:31

When the Bible talks about faith and belief, much more is meant than merely confidence in a certain circumstance (such as "I have faith in gravity," or "I believe the sun will rise tomorrow"). The kind of faith that leads to salvation involves attitudes of your mind (belief), your spirit (trust), and your heart (adoration).

Some skeptics of Christianity believe that faith in Jesus Christ is only for the impressionable, the ignorant, the deluded, the irrational, or the naïve. They say that "faith" requires the willful suspension of intelligence. Nothing could be further from the truth. You are not saved by ignoring facts or the truth. Just the opposite. Faith requires belief (realization and appreciation) in the truth of the gospel—that Jesus is who he said he was, that the Bible is true, and that Christ is the way of salvation.

"Trusting in God" means you have enough confidence in God to give him ownership of your life. You are certain that his plan for you is better than your plan. And you are willing to build your life on that trust.

A sure sign of saving faith is the desire to worship God. Worship is simply the adoration of God, giving him praise and reverent devotion. This rises naturally from an appreciation for the gift of salvation at the great cost of the sacrificial death of Jesus. A response of gratitude to God always flows from true faith.

The sixteenth-century Christian reformer Martin Luther summed up belief and faith with this statement:

Faith is a living, daring confidence in God's grace, so sure and certain that the believer would stake his life on it a thousand times.[10]

God's gift of salvation is waiting for those who believe.

For the Christian, Jesus Is the Only Way to God, Because Jesus Is God

Jesus Christ is at the center of the Christian faith. You have to believe in Jesus if you are going to experience God. Although most people are put off by having only one way to get to God, the hesitancy for most people is that *Jesus* must be the way. This is why the controversies underlying Hillary's initial question center on the theology of Christ.

In the holy hullabaloo that swirls around Jesus, some consider this theological doctrine to be his greatest attraction; others consider it to be a grand offense. The different viewpoints are understandable considering that he claimed to know God. Wait, it was more than that. He claimed to be God. And most controversial of all, he claimed that his death on the cross was the only way a sinful humanity could be forgiven by God and experience eternal life.

Any honest study of the Christian plan of salvation will embroil you in the Jesus debate. It is not possible to look only at the extraordinary part of Jesus without dealing with the controversial part. His teachings, miracles, and resurrection are integrated with his theology. His promises for a life of truth, peace, and meaning were all based on a belief in him . . . not just an intellectual assent of his existence, but a faith that he was the sole solution for humanity's spiritual void.

Every person must take a side in the controversy. You, too, must decide for yourself if Jesus was just a good man, or if he was the God-man and the true way to finding and experiencing God.

QUESTIONS FOR REFLECTION AND DISCUSSION

- Read Galatians 5:11. What does the apostle Paul mean by the phrase "the offense of the cross"?
- Give three reasons why Jesus is and always has been controversial.
- When you take Jesus out of Christianity, what's left?

9

One God, Three Persons? Seriously?

Introduction

I (Stan) was on a short flight I often take for business. During the final descent I learned the woman sitting next to me sold medical diagnostic equipment to hospitals and clinics. She asked me what I did for a living, and I told her I was in Christian publishing. Without skipping a beat, she proudly informed me that her favorite book was *The Shack*. I was curious to know why she liked it so much. "Because it helped me understand God better," she replied pensively.

I had never read the wildly successful book because I listened to the people who had given me their opinions, mostly that the book gave an incorrect (some said heretical) picture of God and the Trinity. But after hearing the heartfelt one-sentence review from the woman on the plane, and believing that it was probably the only Christian book she had ever read, I had to read it.

As I started to read and enjoy *The Shack*, I had to admit that I had avoided the book because I didn't want to disrupt my own preset ideas about the Trinity. I think that's the way it is with many of the doctrines we believe. We get a shallow understanding of something like the Trinity, which invites deeper reflection, and then are quite content to go no further. But in doing so, we deprive ourselves of the opportunity to strengthen our relationship with God by looking at him from a new perspective. And there's no question *The Shack* offers a new perspective.

■ ▮ ■

It's possible you've read *The Shack*, because with more than fourteen million copies sold, it's one of the most popular Christian books of all time. But if you have avoided the book for some reason, we want to provide a quick synopsis since the theme goes to the heart of this chapter.

The Shack is about a father named Mack who experiences a tragedy that severely damages his faith in God. It's only when he is invited to an abandoned shack and encounters God in three persons that his belief takes a dramatic turn. There is Elousia, a large black woman also known as "Papa," or God; a Middle Eastern man dressed like a laborer, complete with tool belt and gloves, whose name is Jesus; and a willowy, ethereal Asian woman by the name of Sarayu, who is the Holy Spirit. Here's an excerpt from *The Shack* describing the first time Mack encounters all three persons:

> Thoughts tumbled over themselves as Mack struggled to figure out what to do. Was one of these people God? What if they were hallucinations or angels, or God was coming later? That could be embarrassing. Since there were three of them, maybe this was a Trinity sort of thing. But two women and a man and none of them white? Then again, why had he naturally assumed that God would be white? He knew his mind was rambling, so he focused on the one question he most wanted answered.
>
> "Then," Mack struggled to ask, "which one of you is God?"
>
> "I am," said all three in unison. Mack looked from one to the next, and even though he couldn't begin to grasp what he was seeing and hearing, he somehow believed them.[1]

The Trinity: "It makes no sense!"

As we wrote this book about the toughest questions people are asking about God and the Bible, young adults were our inspiration. In fact, we decided to write this book for them, for two important reasons. One, there are lots of them. The population now contains a greater percentage of young adults (or millennials, if you prefer) than baby boomers or Gen Xers, and there are more young adults in the workforce than any other group. (Hey, we're not stupid; the bigger the audience, the more books we can sell.)

The other and more important reason we decided to focus on young adults is that they are leaving our churches. Many between the ages of eighteen and thirty-five don't think the church has done a very good job of answering their questions about God and Christianity. This isn't the only explanation, but it's an important and tangible reason they are leaving organized religion in greater numbers than any other group. So we decided to write this book for them. But for our book to have any meaning for our young adult audience, we knew we had to focus on the unanswered questions they are asking.

Chris, who just happens to be a young adult pastor, was an integral part of this process. Over a period of several months, he did a lot of listening, both in a weekly community gathering of young adults and also with individuals over lots of cups of coffee. In addition, he designed a survey that was distributed to approximately one hundred people, asking them for their most important and toughest questions on a variety of spiritual and doctrinal topics.

Much to our delight, they asked dozens of great questions, which we have used as a guide throughout the book. However, for this chapter on the very difficult topic of the three-in-one nature of God—commonly known as the Trinity—we decided to use their questions as our outline. In fact, we're using *all* of the questions they asked about the Trinity. As it turns out, regardless of your age, these are probably your questions as well, because Christians and non-Christians alike have been asking them for a very long time.

Our intention is not to provide standardized answers to these questions, mainly because standardized answers don't cut it. Honestly, of all the topics we've talked about so far, the Trinity is the most challenging because it falls so far out of our normal way of thinking. There are no easy answers, logical explanations, or airtight conclusions to the mystery that is the Trinity. In fact, by the time you finish this chapter, you may very well come to the same conclusion one of the young adults expressed in our survey: "It makes no sense!"

Rather than be frustrated by that conclusion, we hope you will be encouraged. We know, that sounds a little contradictory, but stay with us. Join us as we work through these questions, and you might—just like us—see God in a way you never have before.

QUESTIONS FOR REFLECTION AND DISCUSSION

- Are there any doctrines you believe that you have essentially closed the book on because you've reached a conclusion and aren't really interested in views that might challenge yours? Why is it in our nature to protect our ideas and opinions in this way?
- Have you read *The Shack*? If so, how did it help (or hinder) your thoughts about God?

Question 1: "The word *Trinity* is not in the Bible, so where did it come from? And how do you support it from Scripture?"

Okay, that's really two questions, but they point to the same frustration people have about the Trinity. The Bible never mentions the word, yet we hold this common belief at the core of Christianity that God is one, yet also three persons (somehow). Where did that idea come from?

The simple and best answer is that it came from the Bible. Even though the word *Trinity* never appears in the pages of Scripture, all the building blocks for a doctrine of the Trinity are there (you'll see examples in a minute). It's like a beautiful love song that never explicitly uses the word *love*, but its theme is unquestionably obvious. Just because the word *Trinity* isn't used in the ancient text doesn't mean the doctrine isn't clearly there.

Doctrine sometimes gets a bad reputation because it sounds like something others are trying to cram down your throat (Communists and TV commercials are quite good at this). But doctrine isn't evil. In fact, it's actually quite neutral. Doctrine is simply a framework—scaffolding, if you will—that holds together the elements of a particular belief or theory. Take a house, for example. If you had a living room, a bedroom, a kitchen, and a bathroom, scattered in different places, they wouldn't be of much use. It's only when they are brought together in some kind of order under one roof that they make sense and are actually useful. Where the Christian faith is concerned, doctrine is like a house that brings different elements or ideas found in the Bible into a coherent unity.

In regard to the Trinity, we think it works something like this: Since the actual word is not in the text, we have to ask where the fundamental aspects of the Trinity are found. Where in the Bible are the Father, Son, and Holy Spirit mentioned in the same verse or passage? If we can find these places, perhaps we can begin to see the doctrinal house that helps us think about the Trinity.

Here are some references for you to explore. Take some time to read each passage and write your thoughts about what it says about the Trinity:

- John 14:7
- John 17:9–11
- Romans 5:1–5
- 1 Corinthians 6:11
- 2 Corinthians 13:14
- Ephesians 1:13–14
- 2 Thessalonians 2:13–17
- Titus 3:4–7

We could give more examples, but these should be enough to show how all three persons of the Trinity often appear together in Scripture. And as we will see, that's not because the writers of these Bible passages and books were trying to create a doctrine of the Trinity. Rather, the three persons of God appear together in Scripture because this is who God is. The writers were responsive to the inspiration of the Holy Spirit and faithful to the record of what they knew to be true. Quite simply (but not very easily), the theology of the Trinity arose out of that. The way the Bible "supports" the idea of the Trinity is to tell us the story of who God truly is, and that "telling" reveals a God in three persons.

By the way, as you noticed certain characteristics of God in the passages above, you were (intentionally or not) building a kind of doctrinal framework for the Trinity. But the goal here is not to determine whether your framework was correct or incorrect. In fact, we aren't going to go down that path at all. So don't think in terms of passing or failing a test on the Trinity. Instead, simply focus on what verses and passages like the ones you just read say about God.

QUESTIONS FOR REFLECTION AND DISCUSSION

- How have you thought about the Trinity in the past?
- Who introduced you to the idea of the Trinity, and how did they try to explain it? What was your response?
- What is at least one question you have had about the Trinity that has never been answered to your satisfaction?
- On the other hand, was there ever a time when thinking about the Trinity helped you relate to God in a better way?

Question 2: "Someone came up with the doctrine of the Trinity. Who was it? When did it happen? Why did they do it?"

Actually, it's difficult to pin down a single person, or even a group of people. It's not as though some early Christians, after reading some of the same Scripture verses you just did, had a brainstorming session and drafted a widely accepted doctrine of the Trinity. It actually took the church three centuries to arrive at a cohesive doctrinal framework. Even then, there's never been a time when people have not been puzzled by God's tri-personal nature. But that's not the Trinity's fault. It's our fault because we're thinking about it in the wrong way.

If the Trinity was simply a puzzle to be solved, you would expect church history to include the epic "aha" moment when the smartest guys in the room slapped their foreheads and said, "Eureka! Now we *totally* get it!" But the Trinity is not a puzzle any more than God is a puzzle.

Whether you're trying to unlock the secrets of Sudoku, climb the leader board of Candy Crush, or beat the buzzer on *Jeopardy!*, the idea is to *solve* the puzzle, to beat the game, or to get the final answer. But God isn't solvable. He's not a game, and he can't be found by getting all the answers right. He's not something we can quantify or figure out. We wish he was, because it's in our nature to solve puzzles and figure things out. But that's why our attempts to understand God invariably end up in frustration. We want to solve him—comprehend him completely—but God doesn't exist in the realm of the solvable. He is beyond understanding. Even Saint Augustine, one of the smartest people who ever lived, said, "If you can understand it, it's not God."

So how can we possibly expect to come to grips with who God is? If he's too big to understand, too mysterious to solve, and too complex to comprehend, how do we even begin to know him?

We would like to suggest a different way forward: Stop trying to solve God, and start embracing his mystery. Compared to a puzzle, a mystery is something profound. It invites reflection. A mystery is bigger than your mind. Like it is with love, maybe God doesn't exist to be intellectually dissected or mentally conquered. Maybe he is best known when he is experienced, enjoyed, and held in awe.

Besides, how much of God do we really understand anyway? As much as we think we understand the tri-personal God, the reality is that we understand very little. Now, the good news is that the parts we do understand are enough to allow us to relate to him on a meaningful level. And here's even more good news: We don't have to stop there, because there is an infinite depth to be explored.

Try thinking about the Trinity as a mystery rather than a puzzle. And instead of trying to nail a bunch of culprits for dreaming up the Trinity, as if it were some conspiracy theory, think about it as a true and powerful doctrine that shows just how much bigger and how much more interesting God is than we have ever imagined. Embracing mystery requires humility, but it also opens the door to great discovery.

QUESTIONS FOR REFLECTION

- How do you feel about aspects of God remaining a mystery? Does that give you comfort or produce anxiety? Why?
- Does it bother you that it took three centuries for the church to arrive at a doctrine for the Trinity, and we still struggle to understand it? Explain.
- Explain why it might be better to think of God and the Trinity as a mystery rather than as a puzzle.

Question 3: "How do I explain the Trinity when I can't even understand it myself?"

You have probably heard some illustrations that are supposed to help explain the Trinity. One of the most common examples is the egg. Everyone knows an egg has three elements: the yolk, the white, and the shell. Each element is distinct from the other, yet they all combine to make up an egg. Just like the Trinity, right? Well . . . not really.

Yes, all three elements of the egg make up the egg, but each element by itself isn't an egg. You can't isolate the shell and say, "This is an egg." The next time you have guests for breakfast, try scrambling up a couple of eggshells for them. We guarantee they will think you're one egg short of a full omelet. The shell is part of the egg, but separated from the other two parts, it isn't truly an egg. In contrast, if you isolate Jesus or the Holy Spirit or God the Father and say of each one, "This is God," you would still be right. They are all God, but they are not each other. Jesus is equal to God, but he isn't God the Father. The Holy Spirit is equal to Jesus, but the Holy Spirit isn't Jesus.

In his book *Understanding the Trinity*, the Oxford scholar Alister McGrath, who has a background in science as well as theology, provides a better illustration. Jesus allows us to "sample" God in the same way a sample of air in a container allows us to identify the elements in the atmosphere. The whole atmosphere isn't held in a container of air any more than God is contained only in the person of Jesus. Yet the sample gives us a completely accurate picture of the atmosphere, just as Jesus gives us a completely accurate picture of God (John 14:6–10). McGrath writes:

> Because Jesus *is* God, he allows us to find out what God is like, to have a direct encounter with the reality of God. And because God is not totally identical with Jesus, he remains in heaven, in much the same way the earth's atmosphere remains there, despite the fact that we've taken a small sample of it.[2]

The reality is that God is just too big for us to handle. He's certainly too big for us to fully understand. Knowing this deficiency, God came down to our level and became a human being. In this way, says McGrath, he "makes himself available for us in a form which we can cope with."[3]

The same principle holds true for the Holy Spirit, only in this case the Holy Spirit helps us understand Jesus. Christian doctrine tells us that the presence of the Holy Spirit among the followers of Jesus is the same as the presence of Jesus himself (1 Corinthians 12:12–14, 27; Ephesians 4:15–16). This is what Jesus meant when he told his disciples on the night before he was crucified,

> "I will talk to the Father, and he'll provide you another Friend so that you will always have someone with you. This Friend is the Spirit of Truth. The godless world can't take him in because it doesn't have

eyes to see him, doesn't know what to look for. But you know him already because he has been staying with you, and will even be *in* you!"

John 14:15–17 THE MESSAGE

As you come to better understand this dynamic relationship between God the Father, Jesus the Son, and the Holy Spirit, you will be able to better explain the Trinity. McGrath writes:

To encounter the Son is really to encounter the Father and not some demigod or surrogate. To encounter the Spirit is really to encounter the Son and hence the Father.[4]

QUESTIONS FOR REFLECTION AND DISCUSSION

- Does the uniqueness of the Trinity—or the difficulty of accurately analogizing it with other things—add to or take away from its reality?
- Write out some ways you have encountered God and believed you were dealing with God the Father.
- How about Jesus the Son? How do you relate to Jesus?
- Have you felt the Spirit's presence in your life? Explain as best you can.
- In your encounters with the three persons of God, have you always believed that each one is God, or just a part of God?

Question 4: "What is the importance of the Trinity? What's it for?"

Now we're getting down to the essentials. What *is* the Trinity for? Why did God go to so much trouble to relate to us in this way? To wrestle with this question, we will engage with two other questions inspired by Alister McGrath.

1. When we talk about God, what do we mean: God the Father, God the Son, or God the Holy Spirit?
2. How do we experience this God?

The short answer to the first question is that it depends on context, which is given to us through stories told in the Bible. Here are a few examples: If you're reading about the parting of the Red Sea, where God rescued his people from the hands of Pharaoh and their Egyptian oppressors, then you have a picture of God as a *deliverer*. If you're reading about the crucifixion and resurrection of Jesus, then you're talking about God as *Savior*. And if you're reading in the book of Acts about the fire of the Spirit coming upon the disciples, giving them power to speak in other languages, you're talking about God as *enabler*.

When you talk about any of these stories, you're talking about God. The Trinity gives us a multidimensional picture of God acting in history on behalf of his people, whether Jews in the Old Testament or New Testament believers (all people, Jews and Gentiles, who put their trust in Jesus Christ).

Following this pattern, you could say that the doctrine of the Trinity is a composite picture of the different ways God deals with us. The Trinity affirms that God is active in this world, not some detached deity. Whether we are talking about God the Father, God the Son, or God the Holy Spirit, we are talking about a God who is known for what he does as much as for who he is. A true picture of the Trinity shows God as Creator, God as Savior, and God as a real presence in our lives right now.

The second question—"How do we experience this God?"—is answered by the statement we made in our chapter on Jesus: *Jesus is the answer to the question "Does God care about us?"* We encounter and experience God through the person of Jesus, and the way we experience Jesus is through the Holy Spirit. In fact, here's a beautiful statement you should write down and keep as a bookmark in your Bible to remind you of just how important the Trinity is in your life, and why it matters:

The way I experience God is through the Spirit, who represents Jesus Christ in me so that I may gain access to the Father through him.

- Have you ever thought about the Trinity in this way? Does it change the way you see God?

- Are you most comfortable relating to God as Father, Son, or Holy Spirit?

- What is the value in knowing God as a Trinity, always operating through all three persons? Besides the reasons given above, can you think of any other reasons why God's three-in-one existence matters?

Question 5: "Did God create Jesus and the Holy Spirit, or has the Trinity always existed?"

This question goes to the heart of the doctrine of the Trinity and the divinity of Jesus and the Holy Spirit. Why? Because if God *created* Jesus and the Holy Spirit, they are not equal to God. Created beings are, by nature, subordinate to their creator. And if Jesus or the Spirit were created, subordinate beings, that pretty much changes the heart and soul of Christianity into something very different than it is. So on this question, there's really no wiggle room.

Orthodox Christian belief (that is to say, *correct* belief) is based on this understanding of the Trinity:

- *God eternally and necessarily exists as the Trinity.* The Bible begins with the statement "In the beginning God created the heavens and the earth" (Genesis 1:1). That implies that God existed *before* the universe came into existence. (Obviously. It's very difficult to create something if you didn't exist first.) And according to the Bible, God the Father didn't act alone. It was the tri-personal God who brought everything into being:
  - *God the Father* spoke the universe into existence (Genesis 1; Hebrews 11:3).
  - *God the Son* was the divine agent who carried out God's words (John 1:3; Colossians 1:16; Hebrews 1:2).

    ◦ *God the Holy Spirit* was "hovering over the waters" at the moment of creation (Genesis 1:2; Psalm 33:6).

- *The persons of the Trinity have existed eternally and fully as Father, Son, and Holy Spirit.* Before the universe was created, before Jesus came to earth, and before the Holy Spirit made himself known, the Father has been the Father, the Son has been the Son, and the Holy Spirit has been the Holy Spirit—eternally.

    ◦ God is eternal (Psalm 90:2).

    ◦ Jesus is eternal (John 17:5).

    ◦ The Holy Spirit is eternal (Hebrews 9:14).

- *All three persons of the Trinity are fully God.* This is one of the most mysterious aspects of God, and probably one of the toughest ideas to get our minds around. Yet it's crucial because it anchors the belief that God the Father didn't create the others to carry out his work. Jesus is God and the Holy Spirit is God just as much as God is God. Yet they are not three Gods working independently of one another. That would be *tri-theism*, and an incorrect understanding of the Trinity. They are three *persons* working together, in relationship, as one God.

So how do the three persons of God work together? That's what the next question is all about.

QUESTIONS FOR REFLECTION AND DISCUSSION

- If God did create Jesus and/or the Holy Spirit, what problems (if any) would arise for Christian belief?
- Would it change God's character, Jesus' claims, or the Holy Spirit's work?
- Would it change the way we relate to God, Jesus, and the Holy Spirit?

> • If this profound mystery is real—that God exists (and has always existed) in the divine relationship of the Trinity—how does it impact your thoughts about Jesus, the Holy Spirit, and Christian community?

Question 6: "How do God, Jesus, and the Holy Spirit relate to one another?"

From the Bible it is clear that the Father, Son, and Spirit are all divine (that is, they are all God), yet they are distinct from one another. Several passages of Scripture show this distinctness but also reveal how one person of the Trinity relates to another. This is especially apparent when the Father relates to the Son, but there are also references in which the Holy Spirit relates to the Father and the Son:

- The Father appoints the Son to a place of honor (Psalm 2:7; 110:1).
- The Father, by the Spirit, reveals to his prophets the coming of the Son (Micah 5:2; Isaiah 7:13–14; Isaiah 53).
- The Father and Son know each other (Matthew 11:27).
- The Son doesn't know something the Father knows (Mark 13:32).
- The Word is *with* God, as well as being God (John 1:1–2).
- The Father gave the Son to die for us (John 3:16).
- When Jesus was baptized, the Spirit of God descended like a dove and landed on him, and the Father said, "This is my Son, whom I love; with him I am well pleased" (Matthew 3:16–17).
- Jesus prays to the Father (Mark 14:36).
- Jesus asks the Father to send the Spirit, who is referred to as "another advocate" distinct from Jesus himself (John 14:16).

- Jesus ascends to the Father (John 20:17) and sits down at the right hand of the Father (Mark 16:19; Romans 8:34).

As amazing and mysterious and lofty as all of this is, you may be wondering what it means to you on a practical level. It's great to see how the three persons of God relate to each other, but how do they relate to *us*? We're going to give two incredibly important examples. The first is how all three persons in the Trinity are involved in the process of redemption—that is, rescuing people from a life of sin and hopelessness and making it possible for them to have a life with the tri-personal God. The second is how we see and know what true community is through the example of the Trinity.

First, redemption. Check out the following verses and work your way through the subsequent questions to discover for yourself the role of the Trinity in our redemption.

- Read 1 Corinthians 1:19–29. Describe how God designed his rescue plan. Another way of putting it is this: How did God *author* the plan of salvation?
- Read 1 Corinthians 1:30–2:5. Describe how Jesus figures into the plan. Put another way, how did Jesus *accomplish* the plan of salvation?
- Read 1 Corinthians 2:6–16. Describe the Holy Spirit's role in God's redemption plan. Put in terms of your ongoing relationship with God, how does the Holy Spirit *apply* the plan of salvation?

Next, community. How about when God said, "It's not good for the man to be alone" (Genesis 2:18)? Or when God decided to make a nation for himself (Genesis 12:1–5)? What about when God made laws to show his people how to live, serve, and thrive with one another (Exodus 20; Leviticus), or when Jesus sent his disciples out two-by-two to proclaim the good news and heal (Luke 10:1–23)? And finally, have you read John's glimpse of our glorious future together, when we will "be his people, and God himself will be with them [us!] and be their [our!] God" (Revelation 21:1–5)?

Do you recognize a pattern? In every moment of God's eternal story, his creation is built to live in community. And our communal design is a direct result of God's communal being. He is the Trinity. He exists in community. We were made to do the same. And when we live together in loving, serving, self-sacrificing relationships, we powerfully reflect the very image of God.

God would never ask us to do something that (a) is not good for us, and (b) he is not willing to do, or has not already done, himself. The tri-personal God desires for us to be a family, the family of God. And in so doing we have the opportunity to experience the beautiful dance he has exemplified for all eternity.

QUESTIONS FOR REFLECTION AND DISCUSSION

- Describe what you observed about the Trinity in the passage from 1 Corinthians 1:19–2:16. List at least three ways the Father, Son, and Holy Spirit relate to one another.
- In what way does this change the way you relate to God on a daily basis?
- Does thinking about the Trinity help you see God more personally, or more in the abstract?
- How have you experienced God's good design by living in a family of faith?

Question 7: "Why is the Trinity only in the New Testament? There was a need for all three in the Old Testament, but there was only God."

We have already highlighted the role God, Jesus, and the Holy Spirit had in creation, which is recorded in the Old Testament (Genesis

1:1–2, 26). But this question goes more to the appearances of each person by name in the Old Testament. Are there any?

Obviously, God is large and in charge in the Old Testament, but you won't find any mention of *Jesus* (that is, if you're looking for the name rather than the person). Does that mean Jesus was hanging out in heaven during the Old Testament period until it was time for his grand and glorious earthly arrival on Christmas? Not at all. Even though Jesus didn't appear in human form until the incarnation, his presence was evident in the Old Testament.

The most vivid example is the name *Christ* (which is the title of Jesus, not his last name). *Christ* means "Messiah," or "deliverer." The Old Testament prophets wrote of the Messiah as a human deliverer, a son of David, who was also God:

- In the prophetic books, he is depicted as the servant of the Lord, who suffers to bear the sin of his people (Isaiah 52:13–53:12).
- In the Psalms, David's messianic son is also his Lord (Psalm 110:1).
- During the period of exile, the prophet Jonah writes, "Salvation comes from the Lord" (Jonah 2:9).

The Holy Spirit is a little easier to find by name in the Old Testament, where there is a distinction between God and the Spirit. The most common Hebrew word for *Spirit* means "breath," and it's found more than two hundred times. Some samples:

- The Spirit is the breath by which the Word (Jesus) created the "starry host" (Psalm 33:6).
- God sends the Spirit to do his creative work (Psalm 104:30).
- The Spirit inspired the prophets so they could hear and speak God's word (Ezekiel 2:2).

So appearances of Jesus and the Holy Spirit, as well as God the Father, can be found in the Old Testament. But what about the

Trinity? Are there references to the tri-personal God in a single verse or passage, like we find in the New Testament?

We won't find an instance where the three different persons are mentioned together, but there are several places where a threefold repetition of *Lord* can be found. Consider these majestic verses:

> "The Lord bless you and keep you; the Lord make his face shine on you and be gracious to you; the Lord turn his face toward you and give you peace."
>
> Numbers 6:24–26

> For the Lord is our judge, the Lord is our lawgiver; the Lord is our king; it is he who will save us.
>
> Isaiah 33:22

> "This is what the Lord says, he who made the earth, the Lord who formed it and established it—the Lord is his name."
>
> Jeremiah 33:2

> "Lord, listen! Lord, forgive! Lord, hear and act! For your sake, my God, do not delay, because your city and your people bear your Name."
>
> Daniel 9:19

And then we have the triumphant declaration of the prophet Isaiah, who was given a glimpse into the very throne room of heaven, where the Lord is seated. Surrounding him are magnificent angelic beings who are calling to one another as they proclaim the holiness of each member of the Trinity,

> "Holy, holy, holy is the Lord Almighty; the whole earth is full of his glory."
>
> Isaiah 6:3

We are given another picture of this heavenly setting, with the exact same Trinitarian tribute to the tri-personal God, in the book of Revelation. Once again mysterious, supernatural, and utterly awesome creatures surround the throne of heaven and sing to one another day and night,

> "Holy, holy, holy is the Lord God Almighty, who was, and is, and is to come."
>
> Revelation 4:8

References to the Trinity may be more common in the New Testament, where there's a more complete revelation of the tri-personal God, but sometimes we need to go "old school" and search the depths of the Old Testament for evidence of our wonderful Trinitarian God.

Called to Live Holy Lives

We've painted an awesome picture of the Trinity, because that's the way it is. We're simply reflecting what the Bible and the experiences of people throughout the ages tell us. But how do we personalize these incredible word pictures of a God who surrounds us with his wonder and beauty and majesty?

We think theologian Scot McKnight gets to the heart of the matter when he suggests that we stand "on the greatness of the Trinity" by living holy lives. It isn't by accident that the creatures of heaven sing of God's holiness in triads. God is wholly holy and worthy of our praise. But we don't have to stand on the sidelines and watch God be holy. As McKnight advises, we need to learn what holiness means in all areas of life:

> We need to realize that holiness is not just a call to read the Bible daily, to pray daily, to be faithful attendees of church, to be tith-ers, or to follow any other Christian virtues that have become the essence of Christian living. Holiness is a thirst, a drive to know God in his fullness and an unashamed commitment to obey God whatever it costs and wherever we are. It begins in the morning, directs our path during the day, and leads us to confession and praise in the evening.[5]

179

QUESTIONS FOR REFLECTION

- How has your understanding of the Trinity changed in the course of reading this chapter? How has your appreciation for God changed?
- Are there some areas that are still a mystery to you?
- Can you rest in that uncertainty, or does it make you restless?
- Do you think it's possible to live a holy life before God? Why or why not?

10

Does God Really Care About Me and My Life?

Introduction

I (Chris) have a friend in Austin, another in Los Angeles, and one nearby in Orange County, California, who have all posed some variation of this question in the past year: Does God really care about me and my life?

One friend is a former worship leader and a thoughtful Christian. He's also a recovering alcoholic. He's been sober for six months but is still wrestling through one of the most difficult times of his life. Each day, as he teeters between sobriety and inebriation, he wonders if God cares whether he is dry or drowning. He recently asked me, "If I fall off the deep end again, does God even care?"

Another friend is a new Christian. He is the kind of person I love to talk to because, over the past year, he has taken significant steps of faith and is growing more and more excited about God. And yet—like virtually all of us—there is sin in his life that he can't seem to stop. He wants to. He knows he should. But he feels trapped by it and is unsure of how to stop. And the question that is born out of his new faith and his struggle with sin is a familiar one: "With all that I've done—and keep doing—why would God really care about me and my life?"

My third friend is moving into her late thirties. Although she has lots of friends, a close and loving family, and an affirming and life-giving professional community, she can't seem to shake a deep sense of loneliness. She wonders, in spite of herself, if God loves her. In a long text message conversation, she confided that she doesn't doubt that God loves her. Instead, she wonders if God actually likes her. She feels the support of her friends and family, but what about God's care for her? Where is it, and why doesn't she feel it?

■ ■ ■

We've been Christians a long time, studied the Bible, led ministries in churches, and learned to pray (okay, we're still working on that last one). We've even had the privilege of writing a few Christian books (we're still working on that, as well). Yet in the midst of all that Christian experience, including significant and powerful moments with God and his people, we still wrestle with the kinds of questions Chris's friends are asking.

When things in life go sideways and we endure physical and emotional pain, we find ourselves asking, "*Does* God really care about my life?"

When we are swamped by sin, feel enslaved to terrible choices, and can't seem to obey God if our lives depended on it, we wonder, "*Why* would God really care about me?"

And in those times when God's silence is deafening, the spiritual desert is vast, and our prayers seem pointless, we grumble, "*If* God cares about me, then why don't I feel it?"

These are three parts to one giant (not to mention life-altering) question: "Does God really care about me and my life?" Among all the tough questions about God and the Bible we have been wrestling with, this one may be the toughest, because clearly it's the most personal. After all, its potential answer has ripple effects—good or bad—through all of life. And because this question often includes the two other questions posed by Chris's three friends—"Why would God really care about me?" and "If God cares about me, why don't I feel it?"—we will engage all three. And together we'll see where God takes us!

QUESTIONS FOR REFLECTION AND DISCUSSION

- Do you have friends who have asked questions like this? What have you told them?
- In what ways and for what reason have you asked these questions?
- What role has the church or other Christians played in helping or hurting your efforts to understand God's care for you?
- Have you ever experienced God's care for you, even in a small way?

What Does God Care About?

One way to wrestle with this chapter's questions is to back up a bit and ask a preceding question: "What does God care about in the first place?" In other words, what are the things God pays particular attention to? What does he love most? And do we make the list?

To answer these, we should back up even one *more* step. (Think of it as Googling the definition of a word only to find that the definition includes another word you don't know, so you have to keep up the search. Taking one step forward requires two steps back.) The additional question to ask is, "How do we learn what God cares about?" After all, if there is a God and if he cares about anything, there must be some way to clearly understand what those things are.

Fortunately, the answer isn't as complicated as you might think. In fact, it's fairly simple, because we don't have to uncover a set of statements and principles. All we have to do is look to the person of Jesus of Nazareth, the clearest picture of God and what he cares about.

Jesus' first disciples asked as many questions as we do. In John 14, during one Q&A session, Jesus said, "I am the way, the truth, and the life. No one can come to the Father except through me" (John 14:6 NLT). Unfortunately, we too often stop at this true and frequently quoted verse when we should keep reading. Following this statement, Jesus said, "If you had really known me, you would know who my Father is. From now on, you do know him and have seen him!" (vv. 6–7 NLT).

Perhaps reflecting what we would have asked had we been there that night with Jesus, a disciple by the name of Philip said, "Lord, show us the Father, and we will be satisfied" (v. 8 NLT).

The response of Jesus showed his disciples then, and us now, just exactly what we need to do to discover what God cares about. Here's how Jesus answered Philip:

> "Have I been with you all this time, Philip, and yet you still don't know who I am? Anyone who has seen me has seen the Father! So why are you asking me to show him to you? Don't you believe that I am in the Father and the Father is in me? The words I speak are not my own, but my Father who lives in me does his work through me. Just believe that I am in the Father and the Father is in me. Or at least believe because of the work you have seen me do."
>
> John 14:9–11 NLT

Jesus' followers were asking for help seeing God. Jesus' response was clear: "Want to see God? Just look at me and the works I do." Jesus told them what he's telling us: "If you want to see what God really cares about, look no further than me."

QUESTIONS FOR REFLECTION AND DISCUSSION

- In general, what do you think God cares about?
- What evidence do you have for your answer?
- Do you agree that Jesus is the fullest expression of God's love and care? Why?
- What does that mean to you personally?

God Cares for His People

Unfortunately, we don't have the space to review all of Jesus' acts and teachings. But we can give you a snapshot of some of the "work" Jesus did and what it tells us about God and his love for us.

- Jesus' compassion for the suffering (Mark 5), the sinful (Luke 5:27–31), the straying (Luke 15), and the seeking (Mark 10:17–21) shows us that *God cares about the "least of these"* (Matthew 25:31–46).
- Jesus' excoriation of the Pharisees (the first-century religious elite) shows us that *God cares about love and integrity as much as right living* (Matthew 23).
- Jesus' relationship with God (Luke 6:12) and his teaching and prayers (John 15–17) show us that *God cares about our relationship with him.*

In Jesus, we see what God cares about. But there's more. God has given us another way to know: his written Word, the Bible. All of Scripture—from beginning to end—is about God's mission to rescue and redeem his most prized creation: you and us and all of humankind. All the Bible is about Jesus, and the good news for us as told in the Bible is that Jesus' primary goal was to announce that God's kingdom was present in him, and that he would rescue us from the sin, selfishness, and sorrow that is consuming our world.

As we said in chapter 5, the Bible is not *about* us—but it is definitely *for* us. The Bible shows who God is, what God cares about, and what his overarching story for our lives and the universe really is. Although the Bible doesn't cover every detail of our lives, we can see through its pages that God cares deeply for us.

Imagine how life would change if we truly believed that God loves us. Would we not live with more confidence, less depression, more joy, less image-consciousness, more love, and less selfishness? Oftentimes, our doubts about God's care are not born out of ignorance. Instead, they come out of disbelief. It's not that we don't *know* that God cares; it's that we don't *trust* that God cares.

There is a fascinating and beautiful passage of Scripture tucked in the Old Testament book of Zephaniah that summarizes what we've been talking about:

> "For the Lord your God is living among you. He is a mighty savior. He will take delight in you with gladness. With his love, he will calm all your fears. He will rejoice over you with joyful songs."
>
> Zephaniah 3:17 NLT

These are the very words of God, resounding with God's care, which never wavers. He wants us to remember that even in the midst of our sin and wandering from him, God is with us. We can always count on his delight, care, calming presence, and joy.

QUESTIONS FOR REFLECTION AND DISCUSSION

- What do you feel when you read again—or for the first time—these verses about God's care for you? Does it seem real? Possible? Hard to believe? Doubtful? Take a moment to reflect on your reaction.
- Have you ever known someone—maybe a relative or a friend—who may have done something you didn't like, but you never doubted their care for you?
- What would convince you that God cares?

God Cares for Us When We Need It Most

If you're like us, you most often ask for God's presence and joy when you're in the darkest of circumstances. That's also when the questions asked in this chapter arise the most. "God, do you care for us when cancer grows, tornadoes hit, a child is lost, divorce ravages, and depression sinks us?" "God, do you still care for us when finances tank, friendships turn, and fairness is trounced?"

We've talked about the term *omnipresence*. To review, it's the theological word for the belief that God is always everywhere. It means that God is present with us in every place at every moment no matter what. The Bible is full of examples where God was present, even in the toughest circumstances. He was there at Adam and Eve's darkest moment (Genesis 3), when Joshua faced a dangerous battle (Joshua 1), and when King David walked through the "valley of the shadow of death" (Psalm 23 esv). This is who God is. He promises to be with us now through the Holy Spirit (Matthew 28:20; John 14:15–17), and he will be with us forever (Revelation 21:1–4).

We are not guaranteed a storm-free journey. But God has promised to be with us in the middle of those storms. In fact, if God was not present in our suffering, he would not be present at all. Because of sin—not just our sin, but the sin of humanity—everyone on the planet suffers. At one point or another, suffering, pain, sorrow, fear, and death impact us all. Consequently, if God is not present in our suffering, his promise to always be with us is null and void.

Beyond simply being present, God actually does something. The apostle Paul wrote this encouraging reminder to the church in Corinth:

> Praise be to the God and Father of our Lord Jesus Christ, the Father of *compassion* and the *God of all comfort*, who *comforts us in all our troubles*, so that we can comfort those in any trouble with the comfort we ourselves receive from God.
>
> 2 Corinthians 1:3–4, emphasis added

God cares enough to comfort us in our troubles, and he makes sure our troubles—which are never fun—are also never useless. His comfort in our misery is designed to equip us to comfort others in theirs.

But there's more. (Are you seeing a pattern here?) God cares so much that he not only wants us to recognize his presence in our pain, but also wants us to intentionally turn to him with it.

187

- God implores us to come to him and off-load our burdens from our shoulders to his so that we can experience true rest in our souls (Matthew 11:28–29).

- God directs us to cast our worries on him and taste and live an anxiety-free life. And why? Because he *cares* for us (1 Peter 5:7).

- He provides strength in our times of weakness (Philippians 4:13).

- As we endure a time of need, God beckons us to come and receive his mercy and grace (Hebrews 4:16).

- When we are brokenhearted, God can provide the healing we need (Psalm 147:3).

God Is Empathetic in His Care for Us

Every year Chris leads a weekend retreat with fifteen to thirty young adults. This past fall, the theme of the retreat was inspired by David Platt's book *Radical: Taking Back Your Faith From the American Dream*. On the retreat, as in the book, the young adults were challenged by what Jesus asks his followers. He tells them to deny themselves for his sake (Luke 9:23–25), to give up the things they most love (Mark 10:17–31), and to not look back, for anyone or anything (Luke 9:57–62; Matthew 10:37–39).

This kind of devotion is a tall order for us, yet it is remarkably simple: Love God, follow Jesus, and be led by the Holy Spirit more than anything and everything else in life. If that seems like an impossible task, because of the cultural influences that sweep us up and carry us in the opposite direction, take heart. God isn't asking us to do something he was unwilling to do himself.

Part of the unique and absolute glory of the incarnation is that Jesus experienced—firsthand, in vivid color—everything that we experience. He laughed and cried, ate and hungered, felt pleasure and pain. He was adored and hated, loved and despised, followed and persecuted. He was tempted when tired, abandoned when vulnerable, and murdered when innocent. And because of his personal experience with humanness, his empathy for us is deep and perfect. The Bible puts it well: "This High Priest [Jesus] of ours understands our weaknesses, for he faced all the same testings we do, yet he did not sin" (Hebrews 4:15 NLT).

He is not an impersonal, unfeeling God. He knows what we are going through. And he cares. That care for us is exemplified in the experience of Jesus. After all, why come to this sin-infested cosmic rock at all? Why not sit back and just watch it burn? If we were God, we would probably throw our hands up in the air, say, "Have it your way," and vow to never visit this godforsaken place again. But that's not God's way. "Because of his great love for us, God, who is rich in mercy, made us alive with Christ even when we were dead in transgressions—it is by grace you have been saved" (Ephesians 2:4–5).

God cares for us so deeply, and empathizes with us so truly, that he could not leave us on our own.

QUESTIONS FOR REFLECTION AND DISCUSSION

- Have you ever thought about God's incarnation (becoming human) in this way? How does Jesus' understanding and experience of human life impact the way you think about God caring for you?
- If you were allowed to become God for a few days (yes, we would love that, too!), do you think it would give you better perspective on what it's like to care so deeply for people who don't always care for you in return? What might that feel like?
- What—if anything—would you do to prove your love for them?

But *Why* Does God Care for Me?

We hope that all the questions we wrestle with in this book are refreshing and honest. But few are as honest as the one Chris's friend asked: "With all that I've done—and keep doing—why would God really care about me and my life?" Wrestling with that question faithfully takes us to a subject few people like to talk about, even in our churches: sin.

The word *sin* has fallen out of favor these days. In our culture there is no such thing as sin. There is no absolute right and wrong. We now think of our actions solely as preferences. What is right for me may not be right for you, but it's definitely not sin; it's just *my* preference.

Yet in most of us, there is a deep-seated, naturally occurring sense of inferiority and unholiness when we encounter the holy God of Scripture. It's part of the reason we resist him so much. We know he's right and good and perfect, and as much as we would like to hide or deny it, we know that we are not. Ultimately, we have to face the reality that we are broken, rebellious, and sinful. When we finally come to this point, it can feel like a very dark place. And the question "Why would God love me?" occurs as naturally as the inferior feelings that caused it.

Why would God love us? We discussed part of the answer in chapter 2, but it is worth repeating here. In fact, it is worth repeating *everywhere*. "God is love" (1 John 4:16). For God to powerfully love us is to remain true to who he has always been, who he is, and who he will always be. And it's out of that love—out of his very being—that God caringly acts on our behalf. As God's Word reminds us, there was no greater display of love than the sending of his Son. Here's what the apostle John writes in his letter to first-century believers:

> This is how God showed his love among us: He sent his one and only Son into the world that we might live through him. This is love: not that we loved God, but that he loved us and sent his Son as an atoning sacrifice for our sins.
>
> 1 John 4:9–10

There is an important distinction to make. In these verses, John refers to the *world* in the same way he does in his biography of

Jesus, the gospel of John, specifically in the Bible's most famous verse, John 3:16. When he writes, "For God so loved the world," he uses the word *world* to refer to humanity. This is a specific reference to God's personal love for us, not an amorphous love of everything the world contains, like limestone, cats, mosquitos, and pop music. You are the *object* of God's love, which covers all of humanity, and applies to each of us individually.

In the second half of the verse, John says "that whoever believes in him [Jesus] shall not perish but have eternal life." The *whoever* isn't just anybody. It's you and us and all individuals throughout history who choose to trust Jesus for their salvation.

When you hear that beloved verse, keep in mind that you are his beloved creation. God is not speaking in generalities. He has you in mind. The answer to why God cares about you is found, simply, in his nature. God is love. So God loves.

God's Love Defined

It's important to define *love* here. Love does not mean God will always say yes to everything you want or ask for. It doesn't mean you have to do specific things to earn that love. It doesn't mean that you will always get along with others, or always be happy. God's love is perfect love, which means he desires what is the absolute best for you. Which means he will sometimes say no. He knows better than we do, so he gives better than we would give to ourselves. At times that can feel quite different from the way our culture defines love. But our culture often gets love wrong, whereas God always gets love right.

Because you are God's creation, he delights in you and in loving you. And his desire is that you would delight in him, because he knows that in him and him alone you are truly free, satisfied, fulfilled, at peace, and loved. And though you are wholly unworthy of this kind of love, God loves you where you are. Your role is to simply, humbly, and fully trust and submit to his love. Your response—believing in Jesus, that his death on the cross covered your sin—shifts the scales and brings you out of your sin, placing you in relationship with the holy God who loves you more than you could ever imagine.

Brennan Manning, the brilliant priest and author who was transparent about his own shortcomings, says it better than we can:

> Jesus Christ loves me just as I am, not as I should be. He loves me beyond morality and immorality. He loves me beyond limit, boundary or breaking point, through all the wrong turns I have made in my past, the mistakes, the moral relapses, the detours, the sins. He loves me even when I doubt it, disbelieve it or deny it. His message to me is this: "I cannot stop loving you."[1]

The *extent* of God's love is shown by the *cost* of God's love. He allowed his holy Son to leave the highest heaven so he could become human. He allowed his Son to suffer unfair accusations, beatings, and torture. And he allowed his Son to die an agonizing death for us. With love of this degree, who could ever doubt his care and concern for us?

> What shall we say about such wonderful things as these? If God is for us, who can ever be against us? Since he did not spare even his own Son but gave him up for us all, won't he also give us everything else?
>
> Romans 8:31–32 NLT

QUESTIONS FOR REFLECTION AND DISCUSSION

- Write down the first few words that come to mind in response to this question: "What do you feel when you read or hear that God loves and cares for you this much?" What words did you write down, and what do they say about your belief? Your questions? Your understanding?
- Take a few moments to do something else: Write a short letter to God describing how you feel about his care and love for you. Be honest. It's just you and him.

Why Don't I Feel God's Love and Care?

There is still another question to wrestle with here. But first, let's recap. The incarnation of Jesus and the Word of God show that God cares for his people. He does so empathetically and with our best in mind. He also cares for you individually. But here's the question that lingers, as posed by Chris's third friend introduced at the beginning of this chapter: If it's true that God cares for me, why in the world doesn't it *feel* like it?

This is the kind of question that piques our interest at a heart level. It's a meaningful and vulnerable question, and if it's one of your questions, we wish we could buy you coffee or lunch and talk with you in person. One day, by God's good grace, maybe we can. Until then, a few more words and a few more questions will have to do.

Here are five questions we all need to consider as we wrestle with not feeling that God cares for us:

1. Is it true?

When it comes to our experience of God's love, the first question to wrestle with is not a *feeling* question at all. It's a *thinking* question. While our feelings and experiences are a crucial part of our understanding of love, they are not the only part. We need to ask, "Is God real, and are Jesus' claims true?" Because if they are not, it doesn't matter what we feel.

In a podcast interview, scholar and Anglican priest N. T. Wright was asked to define the gospel. He replied, "This is the gospel: Jesus Christ, who died on a cross and was resurrected, is Lord of all."[2] Dr. Wright's response was clear and succinct. But it seemed to be missing something compared with other definitions we've come to believe. Where's the business about our personal salvation from sin? God's loving sacrifice? Or going to heaven if we believe in him?

As the podcast rolled on, it became quite clear that Wright's answer was simple for a very good reason. If Jesus didn't die on the cross, and was then resurrected, the rest doesn't matter. But if these things did actually happen, then our salvation, God's love, and our belief are very real and eternally effective.

The apostle Paul totally agrees with Wright (actually, it's the other way around):

> If Christ has not been raised, our preaching is useless and so is your faith. More than that, we are then found to be false witnesses about God, for we have testified about God that he raised Christ from the dead. . . . And if Christ has not been raised, your faith is futile; you are still in your sins. . . . If only for this life we have hope in Christ, we are of all people most to be pitied.
>
> 1 Corinthians 15:14–15, 17, 19

If Christ was not raised from the dead, there is no defeat of death and sin. And if there is no defeat of sin and death, Jesus was just a good moral teacher. And if Jesus was just a good moral teacher, it doesn't matter if he cares about us, because he's just another dead philosopher.

But if the gospel *is* true—if it *is* a real, historical, actual event that Jesus of Nazareth walked out of the grave after being crucified—then everything else he said and did matters. If Jesus had the authority to conquer death—the one aspect of human life no human can conquer—then he must be Lord of all. And if he is Lord of all, then he alone knows how life is supposed to be lived. And if he alone knows how life is best lived, he is the one to follow.

As we have shown in this book, we believe that Jesus' life, death, and resurrection were historical and very real. If you agree, your understanding of, belief in, and reflection on this truth will breed in you a deep gratitude to God, which in turn will help you feel God's love and care.

- Why does the resurrection of Jesus matter?
- What's wrong with treating Jesus merely as a wise teacher or dead philosopher?
- How does the risen Christ help you feel God's love and care?

2. Is it sin?

Now, it's possible to believe in the risen Lord and still not feel God's love. In fact, it's *probable* you won't feel God's love if there's something getting in the way of your relationship with him. At the risk of oversimplifying things, we're just going to say it. The reason you may not feel God's love is because you're hanging on to some sin.

There's a kind of cosmic interference in our relationship with God when we sin. Sin in our life disrupts the intimacy in our relationship with God. We're a sinful bunch, too, and we've experienced this sin-caused separation all too often. Perhaps that is why you do not feel God's love for you.

3. Is it disbelief?

Sin has lots of nasty by-products. It breaks our relationship with God, with others, and with his created order. It makes a huge mess. One of those nasty by-products is that we don't believe it's possible for God to actually love us. As we discussed earlier, sometimes we wonder, "How could he love me? I'm such a screw-up." Belief might be the answer. And we don't mean blind faith or uninformed belief. Rather, we think of belief as a door. It's not the final destination, but the door we must go through to reach the destination. In this case, belief is not experience itself, but belief is the door to experience. Some of you, like us, fail to experience God's care and love because you don't believe it's possible.

4. Is it practice?

There is a reason the actions of Christianity are called Christian "practices." Like any other relationship we have ever experienced, we are asked to *do* something. We're not called by God to somehow earn his favor, but to walk with him in relationship. James 4:8 (ESV) says, "Draw near to God, and he will draw near to you." This is a promise you can take to the bank. But you have to actually go to the bank!

5. Are you alone?

One of the confusing aspects of modern Christianity is its emphasis on "personal" salvation, "private" confession, and "individual" Bible study and prayer. Christianity is not like golf, with one guy or girl in plaid pants going at it alone. Christianity is not meant to be practiced in isolation. It's a team sport, like football, with a variety of players, coaches, and fans making success possible.

One of the reasons you may not feel God's care and love for you is because you are disconnected from a group of people—a church, small group, or other kind of Christian community—in which you are truly known and loved. God's love is felt deeply and profoundly when you unselfishly serve others, share your failures and your victories, and receive support and love from the body of Christ. *You were never intended to walk this road alone.* Never. Though it is messy and difficult, once you connect with other followers of Jesus who have given all of themselves to God and his mission in the world, you will experience God's care and love in deep ways. Not only that, but you will also become God's ambassador for *giving* his love to others.

Practicing the Presence of God

We began this book by asking the questions "Is God real, and how can you know?" We hope this is a question you've been able to address in ways that are helpful, if not life changing. Remember, belief isn't about absolute certainty. It's about trust in a God who has made himself known in our world, through his written Word, and in the person of the living Word, Jesus Christ.

Yet even belief grounded in the reality of who God is and what he has done for us isn't completely satisfying—not if our belief in God is all we have. We need to believe that God is truly with us, not just that he is real. As pastor and popular author John Ortberg says,

> To believe as Jesus did doesn't just mean believing that God exists. It means to believe he's always present.[3]

In fact, Jesus is the complete expression of "God with us" (Matthew 1:23). He lived his life in the presence of God the Father, and he wants us to have the same experience. We know, it seems impossible, given our earthly temptations, distractions, pressures, and worries. But that's exactly why we need to seek God's presence, so God can help us deal with all of it.

Jesus is no longer with us in his physical person, but we can still experience Jesus in all his fullness through the Holy Spirit. On the night he was betrayed, Jesus asked God to give his disciples the Holy Spirit, who would be God's presence with us forever:

> "And I will ask the Father, and he will give you another advocate to help you and be with you forever—the Spirit of truth. The world cannot accept him, because it neither sees him nor knows him. But you know him, for he lives with you and will be in you."
>
> John 14:16–17

Stop and reflect on this for a moment. The tri-personal God— Father, Son, and Holy Spirit—is present in you. It's not something you can earn or manipulate. If you have put your faith in Jesus by accepting what he did for you on the cross, Jesus is your first Advocate before the Father (1 John 2:1), and the Holy Spirit is your second Advocate. He is quite literally the presence of Jesus in you. To experience God's presence in this way is to rest in him and experience all he is, all he has done for you, all he is accomplishing in you now, and all he has promised to do in the future.

Even if you still have doubts and questions—and we hope you do—you can taste and see that God is good by asking him to be present in your life. We don't have all the answers, but this is something we are sure about: If you continue to sincerely seek him, God the Father, God the Son, and God the Holy Spirit will work in your life as you continue your journey of faith.

QUESTIONS FOR REFLECTION AND DISCUSSION

- Describe a time when you experienced the presence of God in your life.
- Did you consider this an exception to your everyday life as a Christ follower? Why or why not?
- Do you believe it's possible to experience God's presence more often?
- How has this chapter encouraged you to think that way?

Notes

Chapter 1: Is God Real, and How Can You Know?

1. Quoted in Rod Dreher, "Confessions of an Ex-Evangelical, Pro-SSM Millennial," The American Conservative, February 27, 2014, http://www.theamerican conservative.com/dreher/ex-evangelical-pro-gay-millennial.

2. C. S. Lewis, *God in the Dock* (Grand Rapids, MI: William B. Eerdmans, 1972), 108–109.

3. Tim Keller, *The Reason for God: Belief in an Age of Skepticism* (New York: Dutton, 2008), 141.

Chapter 2: Why Did God Create Us?

1. Stanley Grenz, *Theology for the Community of God* (Grand Rapids, MI: William B. Eerdmans, 2000), 100–101.

2. Ibid., 101.

3. Ibid.

4. Ibid.

Chapter 3: Why Doesn't God Make Himself More Obvious?

1. Wayne Grudem, *Systematic Theology: An Introduction to Biblical Doctrine* (Grand Rapids, MI: Zondervan, 1994), 188.

2. Mike Erre, *Astonished: Recapturing the Wonder, Awe, and Mystery of Life With God* (Colorado Springs: David C. Cook), 43–46.

Chapter 4: Can I Trust What the Bible Says About God?

1. Mike Erre, *Why the Bible Matters: Rediscovering Its Significance in an Age of Suspicion* (Eugene, OR: Harvest House Publishers, 2010), 49.

2. Ibid., 51.

3. G. K. Chesterton, *What's Wrong With the World?* (New York: Dodd, Mead and Company, 1910), under "The Unfinished Temple," http://www.gkc.org.uk /gkc/books/1717-h.htm.

4. Peter Leithart, "What Is the Bible For?", First Things, May 18, 2012, http:// www.firstthings.com/web-exclusives/2012/05/what-is-the-bible-for.

Chapter 5: If the Bible Is So Important, Why Is It So Hard to Understand?

1. Henrietta Mears, *What the Bible Is All About* (Ventura, CA: Regal Books, 1983), 20.

2. C. S. Lewis, "Myth Became Fact," in *God in the Dock* (Grand Rapids, MI: William B. Eerdmans, 1970), 63–67.

3. *The Economist*, "The Battle of the Books," December 19, 2007, http://www .economist.com/node/10311317.

Chapter 7: Is Jesus God?

1. Josephus, *Jewish Antiquities, Books 18–19* (Cambridge, MA: Harvard University Press, 1965), 18.3.3 Section 63.

2. Adapted from Bruce Bickel and Stan Jantz, *I Can't See God Because I'm in the Way* (Eugene, OR: Harvest House, 2009), 24–25.

3. Scot McKnight, "Who Is Jesus? An Introduction to Jesus Studies," in *Jesus Under Fire: Modern Scholarship Reinvents the Historical Jesus*, ed. Michael J. Wilkins and J. P. Moreland (Grand Rapids, MI: Zondervan, 1995), 55.

4. Ibid., 56–61, adapted.

5. William Lane Craig, "Rediscovering the Historical Jesus: Presuppositions and Pretensions of the Jesus Seminar," accessed August 22, 2015, http://www .leaderu.com/offices/billcraig/docs/rediscover1.html.

6. C. S. Lewis, *Mere Christianity,* (New York: Touchstone, 1996), 56.

7. Interviewed by Lee Strobel, *The Case for Christ: A Journalist's Personal Investigation of the Evidence for Jesus* (Grand Rapids, MI: Zondervan, 1998), 145–147.

Chapter 8: Why Do Christians Say Jesus Is the Only Way to God?

1. *Wikipedia*, s.v. "Religious pluralism," accessed October 3, 2015, https:// en.wikipedia.org/wiki/Religious_pluralism.

2. Ibid.

3. Ibid.

4. Ibid.

5. Augustine, *On Christian Doctrine* (New York: Pearson, 1958), II.18.

6. John Calvin, *Calvin's Commentary on Titus 1:12*, accessed October 15, 2015, http://biblehub.com/commentaries/calvin/titus/1.htm.

7. William Lane Craig (May 12, 2009). *How Can Christianity Be the One True Religion?* [Video File]. Retrieved from https://www.youtube.com/watch?v=ANk JrynhEzo.

8. Craig Hazen, "Aren't All Religions Basically the Same?" in *The Apologetics Study Bible* (Nashville: Holman Bible Publishers, 2007), 566–567.

9. Dennis Rogers, *Growing Up Into Him* (Duluth, GA: Georgia Baptist Convention, 2012), accessed September 29, 2015, http://www.gbcpublications.org /weeklydevotions/growing-week45.pdf.

10. Martin Luther, *Commentary on Romans*, trans. J. Theodore Mueller (Grand Rapids, MI: Zondervan, 1954), xvii.

Chapter 9: One God, Three Persons? Seriously?

1. William P. Young, *The Shack* (Newbury Park, CA: Windblown Media, 2007), 87.

2. Alister McGrath, *Understanding the Trinity* (Grand Rapids, MI: Zondervan, 1988), 125.

3. Ibid.

4. Ibid, 129.

5. Scot McKnight, *1 Peter: The NIV Application Commentary* (Grand Rapids, MI: Zondervan, 1996), 138.

Chapter 10: Does God Really Care About Me and My Life?

1. Brennan Manning, "Abba I Belong to You," accessed October 10, 2015, http://endeavorleadership.com/quotes-Manning.html.

2. N. T. Wright, "Simply Jesus," *The N. T. Wright Podcast*, audio, August 18, 2013, https://itunes.apple.com/us/podcast/the-n.t.-wright-podcast/id447840163.

3. John Ortberg, "Getting Good at Prayer Isn't the Point," *Leadership Journal* online, Summer 2015, http://www.christianitytoday.com/le/2015/summer-2015 /getting-good-at-prayer-isnt-point.html.

After graduating from college as a theater arts major, **Bruce Bickel** entered the entertainment industry as a stand-up comedian. But his show-biz career was short-lived because he wasn't very funny. Like most failing comedians, he became a lawyer—a profession in which he is considered hilarious. Bruce preaches sermons quite often (but never at a church, just in his spare bedroom).

Stan Jantz has spent his entire professional career selling, publishing, and writing Christian books. Writing is his favorite book activity, because he gets to do it with his longtime coauthor, Bruce Bickel. Together Bruce and Stan have written 75 books with more than 3.5 million copies sold. They have plenty of spare time to write because neither of them has a hobby (much to the chagrin of their wives).

When he's not writing, Stan serves as the executive director of the Evangelical Christian Publishers Association. He loves this job because he gets to spend time with publishing leaders who have the audacity to think they can change the world through Christ-centered books. Stan thinks they may be on to something.